Six Critical Essays on Film

A College Guide for Film Appreciation

Six Critical Essays on Film

A College Guide for Film Appreciation

Mike Kimmel
Foreword by Dr. Henry Hoffman

Copyright © 2019 Mike Kimmel

All rights reserved.

No portion of this book may be reproduced or transmitted in any form or by any means, electronic or mechanical, including photocopying, recording, or by any information storage or retrieval system, except for the inclusion of brief quotations in reviews.

ISBN 13: 978-0998151359

Ben Rose Creative Arts
New York - Los Angeles

Printed in the United States of America
First Edition

Publisher's Cataloging-in-Publication Data provided by Five Rainbows Cataloging Services

Names: Kimmel, Mike, author. | Hoffman, Henry, writer of foreword.

Title: Six critical essays on film : a college guide for film appreciation / Mike Kimmel ; foreword by Dr. Henry Hoffman.

Description: Los Angeles, CA : Ben Rose Creative Arts, 2018.

Identifiers: ISBN 978-0-9981513-5-9 (paperback) | ISBN 978-0-9981513-6-6 (epub ebook) | ISBN 978-0-9981513-7-3 (mobi ebook)

Subjects: LCSH: Motion pictures. | Motion pictures–Reviews. | Motion pictures–Appreciation. | Motion pictures--Evaluation. | Film criticism. | BISAC: PERFORMING ARTS / Film / History & Criticism. | PERFORMING ARTS / Film / Guides & Reviews. | PERFORMING ARTS / Film / Reference. | SOCIAL SCIENCE / Media Studies.

Classification: LCC PN1995.9.E9 K56 2018 (print) | LCC PN1995.9.E9 (ebook) | DDC 791.43/75–dc23.

Praise for
<u>Six Critical Essays on Film</u>

"Mike Kimmel scores again with his <u>Six Critical Essays on Film</u>. This book, packed with critical information, hits a home run for students, fans and professionals. It truly provides an awareness to the details of filmmaking.

After more than 60 years across the landscape of cinema, it is truly a pleasure to read, learn and be entertained through these writings."

– William Wellman Jr.
  Actor of over 200 movies, television shows, documentaries;
  Producer of films and the award-winning documentary,
  <u>Wild Bill Hollywood Maverick;</u>
  Author of <u>The Man And His Wings</u> and <u>Wild Bill Wellman: Hollywood Rebel</u>

"Mike Kimmel gives the film student and film buff a look way behind the scenes as to how these objects of our admiration have been created. If you want to be in the film industry or if you want to learn how it's done, this is a must read."

– Barton Goldsmith, Ph.D.
   Author of the Emotional Fitness and 100 Ways book series.
   Columnist for The Chicago Tribune and Tribune Media.

"Six Critical Essays on Film is a useful guide for college students majoring in fields outside of the arts – particularly the hard sciences, economics, finance, and business. This book offers a common-sense, analytical approach to watching movies with a critical eye. Students will learn to evaluate the relative strengths and weaknesses of films in much the same way that a financial expert analyzes a business plan or profit and loss statement."

– Barry Moltz
   Small Business Expert and Business Author
   Shafran Moltz Group, LLC.
   Author, Bounce, Getting Unstuck,
   Small Business Hacks: 100 Shortcuts to Success

"I am one of those film watchers who used to just sit back and let it all happen. However, I am also trained in hard sciences so it was particularly gratifying that <u>Six Critical Essays on Film</u> could explain the "how" and "why" of choices made by the filmmakers. In other words, it sparked an interest in me to think about what I am watching beyond the story. Mike has become a great teacher, especially for younger students."

   – Michael Kahn
   Financial Markets Columnist
   Author, <u>A Beginner's Guide to Charting Financial Markets</u>

"Mike Kimmel's look at six classic films is a masterpiece. The insights he provides give college students such a thorough perspective on the films that will only enhance their understanding and appreciation. Mike is able to provide such a high level of insight and detail that usually would only be experienced through a graduate level college course on filmography. After reading Mr. Kimmel's book the readers will be able to appreciate these films much more through the knowledge gained and having been equipped with a critical lens."

   – Emilio Urioste Jr.
   Director, Adult Education
   Burbank Adult School, Burbank, California

"Mike's insightful look at the six films provides a unique perspective for college students to analyze things that are typically overlooked. Reading the essays reminded me somewhat of watching a DVD with the director's commentary turned on, but Mike takes it ten steps further by analyzing every distinct aspect. Even if you've seen the films, the awareness provided by his thought-provoking details will leave you no other choice than to see them once or twice more. This is not a book … it is a series of adventures."

> – Tina Guillot
> Toastmasters International District Director, 2016-2017
> Contributing Author, <u>101 Great Ways to Compete in Today's Job Market</u>

"What a wonderful way for the reader to discover the techniques, and the particular uses of camera work that were used in the black and white – as well as the modern-day – feature film. One who has viewed film quickly, hurrying through the plot, not noticing the director's actions and nuances that amaze is cheated. Mike urges the reader to study the film with him, ultimately leading him by the hand through each marvelous device."

> – Beverly Wellmeyer
> Assistant Professor of Graphic Arts
> Delgado Community College,
> New Orleans, Louisiana

"Mike Kimmel's latest writing adventure into speaking about art to young people is his best yet. Mike is driven by his own love and work in theatre and film to share its spirit and creativity with our next generations of both practitioners and fans. His motive is a simple one: to help others understand and love the art behind cinema. With his <u>Six Essays</u>, he does just that. Mike's own professional career has now opened him up to the world of teaching and sharing of ideas and practice. This book will be an excellent primer for the young film-goers and the young filmmakers who will make their own contributions to America's cultural and artistic future."

   – Stephen Morrow
     Professor of English and Humanities
     Oklahoma City Community College,
     Oklahoma City, Oklahoma

"Mike Kimmel has written the ultimate guide to writing that pesky 'how does one say it' film appreciation and review essay. So much so I'd like to go back to school because I'd have the tools. And the essays are wonderful. I defy you to not want to go and watch the films."

   – Susannah Devereux
     Actor, <u>Iron Thunder</u>, <u>Jimmy Zip</u>, <u>Chasing Ghosts</u>, <u>Chronology</u>, <u>Fogg</u>, <u>Silver Twins</u>, <u>Those People</u>, <u>Opposite of Earnest</u>
     Portrayed Diane Neilson in <u>Shortland Street</u>,
     South Pacific Pictures for Television New Zealand

"Six Critical Essays on Film guides the reader through a journey of reflection and critical thinking. Oftentimes, audiences simply receive a film as the finished product without a true appreciation and understanding of all the moving parts that make it complete. Like an orchestra with many instruments, film has many important components. Thank you, Mike Kimmel, for shining a light on the mechanics of the art! This book is a solid addition to any filmmaker's library. It will be an invaluable resource to help college students gain a greater understanding and appreciation for the art, craft, and business of feature film."

– GiGi Erneta
Actor, Radio and TV Host, and Writer
Happy Death Day, Happy Death Day 2U,
Flag of My Father, Scandal, Veep,
American Crime, The First, The Purge,
Nashville, Dallas, Jane the Virgin,
Veronica Mars, Roswell, New Mexico

"Author Mike Kimmel has done it again. After a series of groundbreaking books for aspiring young actors, he has set his sights on collegiate filmmakers with this insightful and refreshing look at six classic films. He offers a unique and much needed focus on how casting and actor character choices have contributed to these film giants and their monumental commercial and critical success. In today's often tent-pole CGI film atmosphere, this work is a potent reminder of how character driven material in the hands of carefully selected artists combine to create what is truly and forever classic. A must read for all film students."

– Jean Carol
  Adjunct Professor,
  Media Entertainment Arts Department,
  College of the Canyons,
  Valencia, California
  Emmy Award winning broadcast producer/writer/host for PM Magazine
  Emmy nominated actress for CBS-TV's The Guiding Light
  SAG Cast Award recipient for the feature film Argo.

"I would apply to these essays the same words Mike Kimmel used to praise Casablanca: his film analyses are 'communicated beautifully and with painstaking care.' Kimmel proves by example that academic probing doesn't reduce great films to textbook science. His film dissections burst with enthusiasm, insight and vibrancy. They left me eager to watch the films he discussed, and I did! Including movies that I'd never before considered "must sees." It was a thrill to identify the details I'd read about, like surreal, rain-drenched light-scapes in Taxi Driver and split-screen visual humor in Annie Hall. Better yet, with Kimmel's essays as blueprints, I felt equipped to do my own sleuth work. Analyzing cinematic elements made movie watching a deeply satisfying experience. As a newbie in the art of film analysis, I feel not only newly proficient, but newly addicted.

Ultimately, the beauty of this book isn't the eloquent writing or superb analyses, though there's plenty of both. It's the remarkable way in which, through his warm and inviting words, Kimmel makes room for each reader's creativity, intelligence and talent. He makes a convincing case that we too can write analytical essays that'll do justice to our favorite movies!"

– Eva C. Nusbaum
  Two-Time President,
  New Orleans Toastmasters
  Toastmasters International, District 68

"I have learned information is not effective unless it's priority to the project. Concentrated information is confusion. For anyone who wants to understand the film industry, my advice is to go to an individual who is battle-tested and battle-proven. Have you ever been to skid row? There are geniuses laying in the gutter with all kinds of degrees. You can plaster your walls and mine with their degrees and diplomas. They're a library of information. And they can speak about their fields of expertise very eloquently. But remember – well done is better than well said. Learn from the people who can get it done rather than people who talk about it. Michael is battle-tested and battle-proven."

> – Sammy Maloof
> Hollywood Stuntman
> The Fast and the Furious, 2 Fast 2 Furious,
> Wild Wild West, Rush Hour, Three Kings,
> Gone in 60 Seconds, Spiderman 2,
> Transporter 2, Déjà Vu, Angel, Firefly,
> Burn Notice, Baywatch, Enemy of the State,
> Charlie's Angels, Entourage, Miami Vice

"Having used Mike Kimmel's monologue and scene books in my acting classes for years, I trust Mike's unique abilities to provide excellent resources for students as well as instructors. His newest offering, <u>Six Critical Essays on Film</u>, serves as a uniquely valuable asset to the tool box of college students and their instructors – or anyone who wishes to embark on in-depth evaluation of classic and contemporary films."

– Sharon Garrison
  Actor, Producer, Acting Coach, and College Instructor
  <u>Claws</u>, <u>Preacher</u>, <u>Game of Silence</u>, <u>Salem</u>, <u>American Horror Story</u>, <u>Bomb City</u>
  Portrayed Judge Amelia Sanders in AMC's <u>Drop Dead Diva</u>
  Adjunct Professor, Texas Woman's University, Texas Christian University, Tarrant County College

"This is a book for students seriously 'thinking' about film. Kimmel helps you dissect this complex media, with six prime examples designed to unveil the major components that make a movie a masterpiece. He shows us how to look at movies with a critical and analytical eye, allowing us to discover the many different aspects of brilliant filmmaking. It gives us not only a new appreciation for the artistry, but a new, enhanced enjoyment of the art – and of simply watching and enjoying movies."

— Stephen Bowling,
President, The Prometheum Foundation
Stamford, Connecticut
Author, <u>My Life List,</u>
<u>Calvin the Christmas Tree</u>

For my Mother and Father

"The first star of a motion picture should be its story."

– Cecil B. DeMille

Table of Contents

Praise for <u>Six Critical Essays on Film</u>	v
Foreword by Dr. Henry Hoffman	xxiii
Acknowledgments	xxix
Introduction	xxxi
A Note on Style	xliii
Genius Acting and Directing in <u>The Gold Rush</u>	1
Ideology in von Sternberg's <u>Blonde Venus</u>	11
Anatomy of a Masterpiece: <u>Casablanca</u>	21
Light and Movement in <u>Taxi Driver</u>	41
Editing Brilliance in <u>Annie Hall</u>	51
<u>Star Wars</u>: The Story is Star	59
Afterword	69
A Simple Technique for Improving College Essays	71
Appendices	73
Works Cited	75
Recommended Reading	77
Must-See Movies	81

Mike Kimmel

A Brief Glossary of Film Terms   89
About Henry Hoffman   97
About Mike Kimmel   99

Foreword

In his practical and witty book <u>Writing Without Bullshit</u>, Josh Bernoff, a renowned technology analyst, says that at the center of good writing is what he calls the Iron Imperative, or treating the reader's time as more valuable than your own. In his fine new book of essays on films that have made a profound difference in his life, Mike Kimmel embraces this tonic of making every word count, reminding us of Mark Twain's keen insight that the difference between the right word and the almost right word is the difference between lightning and a lightning bug.

The film selections reveal a catholicity of tastes: they are liberal, but comprehensive. The writer references Louis Gianneti's excellent <u>Understanding Movies</u>, and other film textbooks for inspiration, alignment and wordplay. Like him, the writer outlines the narrative of the film, concentrating on key plot reversals, all-the-while highlighting with precise decision-making salient examples of the filmmaker's cut-to-the-guts choices, inducing a jam-thrust to the reader's imagination towards learning how to *read* a film, a happy amalgam of technology and meaning.

Mike Kimmel

The writer opens up his critical witness with an endorsement of The Gold Rush and Charlie Chaplin, whom George Bernard Shaw dubbed "the premier artist of the motion picture screen." The writer says that Chaplin's essential sweetness offers an effective counterpoint to "the danger and violence that pervades much of the film." Digressing on the early innovators in film, Stanley Kubrick said that if you want to see emotion played to the hilt, watch Chaplin; if you want form, pure space in front of you, Eisenstein is your man. But having been trained in vaudeville, Chaplin's aesthetic was film as theatre (with a further conviction that humor had the capacity to take on almost any controversial issue). To this end, he told his cameraman to point the lens toward the Tramp and the rest would take care of itself. The writer does convince us, though, that Chaplin did "stage scenes with a high degree of complexity." In summarizing Chaplin's epic status in the history of film, the director Bernard Bertolucci has the last word: Calvaro's death in Chaplin's Limelight (1952), when they place the white sheet over his lifeless form, is a metaphor: "…pulling the motion screen itself over Charlie Chaplin—the death of cinema."

Josef von Sternberg's Blonde Venus is exposed by the writer as surfacing agitations in a deeper ocean, despite (quoting Gianneti) "an added complication of any ideological analysis involves period and historical context." Eisenstein said a film says more about the time in which it was made rather than the time it is attempting to depict. But von Sternberg valorized Helen, played by the incomparable Marlene Dietrich, and allowed for her to both revel and coolly dwell in the special allure of the feminine role in the competiveness of male territory. Even as Helen continues to combat those men who create her suffering, and then conversely admire her for taking it on, von Sternberg moves towards an archetype of a new species of female.

With Martin Scorsese's Taxi Driver, the writer meticulously unlocks the director's texture of genuine hardship for an antihero, played with a ruthless nihilism by Robert De Niro inside a world of thick death under an anguishing dark sky. Travis generates his own self-importance, even as he resists letting go of something that was over and done with moments ago. He cannot seem to move without slithering, until in the end he releases, like a bitter shepherd, his stuffed explosives, gaining a cockeyed redemption against all odds.

The centerpiece of the book is the writer's affirmation of Casablanca as a film that achieves a sustained level of excellence, an alchemy of grand intentions and moments of splendor, its requisite placement of exaltation in all the right places: acting, directing, editing, screenplay.

With Woody Allen's <u>Annie Hall</u>, the writer explores the creative freedom of the editing choices. I remembered what Ralph Rosenblum said, he who (indeed) cut the film, in his book <u>When the Shooting Stops, the Editing Begins</u>, that when he and the Woodman ran the first draft of the film, they decided to focus only on the unique relationship between Alvy and Annie as the central arrow of intention, and let the other back-stories fall to the cutting-room floor. In reading the writer's penetrating survey of Allen's comedic <u>leit-motifs</u>, or recurring themes, I was also reminded of Mike's own talent in this art form, which somebody once described as for those who think. (Tragedy is for those who feel.) Takes one to know one.

The final essay is a discursive unlocking of the cultural impact of George Lucas' <u>Star Wars</u>, which generated a rebirth of the sci-fi genre: "… he has effectively created a new … reality that has captured the imagination of movie fans worldwide."

Finally, I would say that what emerges from Mike Kimmel's aggregate of essays is a free-associative mode that is also intense. A feeling comes through that he needs *must* write about these films, because he wants to make a connection with strangers, those who are like-minded in hopefully sharing his love of film. Finally, what Mike's achievement does is to support Stanislavski's observation that the critic is the artist's best friend.

Dr. Henry Hoffman
New Orleans, Louisiana

Acknowledgments

As always, a million thanks to Mollie, Adele, and Tammy, my three wonderful sisters. Their kindness, graciousness, and generosity are beyond description and beyond compare.

Many thanks to Kimberly Bliquez, GiGi Erneta, Tina Guillot, Stephanie Knights, Aurora Medina, Eva Nusbaum, Karen Pavlick, Jan Sutton, Erik Beelman, Stephen Bowling, David Breland, Francis Ford Coppola, Michael Kahn, Gene LeBell, Barry Moltz, Sammy and Jennifer Maloof, Ben McCain, Jim and Angela O'Doherty, Morgan Roberts, Ben Rose, and William Wellman Jr. for their encouragement, support, inspiration, and unwavering loyalty.

Very special thanks to Dr. Henry Hoffman for sharing his knowledge and insights in the foreword to this book. Dr. Hoffman has mentored thousands of performing artists through all different stages in their careers – and has been a dynamic and energetic advocate for arts education worldwide. His passion for education and the performing arts has been a tremendous source of inspiration to me through the many years of our friendship, camaraderie, and collaboration.

Introduction

In the modern age, film may be called the universal language of human experience. Academy Award winning writer-director-producer Francis Ford Coppola says it best: "movies are the art form most like man's imagination." Most people would be hard-pressed, in fact, to find friends, colleagues or co-workers who do not enjoy stretching their collective imaginations with trips to the cinema.

The deeper we delve into any subject, of course, the more interesting it becomes for us. The visual and performing arts are no exception. The arts, however, largely due to their abstract nature, present a unique challenge for adult learners. Film, in particular, is an area of study that is often problematic for college and university students. Almost everyone enjoys watching films – both at home and in commercial movie theaters. Reviewing, evaluating, and writing critically about feature films, however, is quite another matter entirely – and often proves daunting for students throughout their academic careers.

Given this, it is interesting to note how diehard film aficionados approach their own personal experiences at the multiplex. The late, great Chicago film critic Roger Ebert was fond of viewing films multiple times. "Every great film," Ebert said, "should seem new every time you see it." What Ebert meant, I believe, is that we gain a broader appreciation for our favorite films by viewing them multiple times and identifying different components that work well at every new screening.

Entrepreneur Patrick Bet-David not only enjoys going to the movies, but applies the experience in a very practical manner. Bet-David recently revealed that he often goes to movie theaters early in the day by himself and watches films analytically for creative ideas. He then searches for ways to apply those ideas to his many successful and diverse business ventures.

Both approaches may be different, but are indicative of the high regard – and fundamental importance – of the position films occupy in our modern culture. It is appropriate, therefore, to train ourselves to evaluate films with great care and specificity, and in a manner fully congruent with their stature and relevance.

This book is by no means a comprehensive analysis of film. Instead, it is a brief collection of essays on six movies that have long been personal favorites. Recognize, too, that there are many different criteria with which to evaluate motion pictures. Acting, directing, cinematography, lighting, movement, sound, music, dialogue, storyline, ideology, historical context, setting, and locale are among the most common elements we can isolate, analyze, and dissect.

The six films selected for this book exemplify the most active and dynamic components of great motion pictures. In focusing attention on these six movies, certain key concepts emerge clearly – and scream out to be recognized, discussed, and evaluated in depth. Specifically, acting and directing (<u>The Gold Rush</u>), story (<u>Star Wars</u>), movement (<u>Taxi Driver</u>), editing (<u>Annie Hall</u>), and ideology (<u>Blonde Venus</u>) are most clearly evident throughout these five terrific examples. The sixth offering, however, <u>Casablanca</u>, is another type of film entirely. <u>Casablanca</u> is a true masterpiece, and succeeds in practically every manner one might wish to measure a movie. There are so many diverse elements working together well, in fact, that it becomes difficult to curtail our discussion. The essay on <u>Casablanca</u>, therefore, is substantially longer than the rest.

To begin, let's consider the ways in which acting contributes to a film's success. If you admire an actor in a certain film role, then stop, think and try to explain exactly why you do. In writing about an actor, we may point to specific details of that actor's performance. Being as precise as possible here will really help you – and will definitely help your writing. What particular actions does the actor perform well? What emotions does this actor portray convincingly? You can also start thinking very creatively – by imagining other films, roles, and genres in which this actor would be similarly effective.

As an example, take a look at the discussion of supporting actors Tom Murray and Mack Swain in the essay on Charlie Chaplin's <u>The Gold Rush</u>. Specific scenes are described for the reader. Specific actions these actors perform in those scenes are evaluated, as well. Moreover, the size and physicality of both men contrast well with Chaplin's relatively smaller stature, a recurring theme throughout the maestro's brilliant career.

We may also discuss the creative casting process in film – specifically with Mark Hamill as <u>Star Wars</u>' Luke Skywalker and Peter Lorre as Señor Ugarte in <u>Casablanca</u>. The casting of these two actors – one, a star, and the other a relative unknown at the time – played a subtle, but significant role in the success of these two films. Casting is discussed in detail in their respective essays. Peter Lorre was already a major star, while Mark Hamill was a relative unknown. Casting these two actors contributed to the effectiveness of <u>Casablanca</u> and <u>Star Wars</u> in two wildly different ways. The casting analysis offered in these two chapters is a guideline you can follow in your own film essays and critiques.

Actor casting is a component of film that is generally overlooked in academic writing for film appreciation classes. A thoughtful discussion, then, of casting choices – and the casting process in general – will no doubt win points for you with your college professors. Ultimately, in all three films, the actors deliver something unique and memorable on screen. Their performances add immeasurably to the success and overall impact of their films in specific ways we can analyze and reflect upon in our essays.

Try this exercise with me. We can add an additional layer of complexity to actor analysis by considering popular films from prior years – and imagining our favorite modern day actors playing roles in those projects. Imagine Brad Pitt and George Clooney, for example, playing the Sean Connery and Michael Caine roles in <u>The Man Who Would Be King</u> for director John Huston. Imagine Scarlett Johansson taking a trip back in time to 1946 – and stepping into Rita Hayworth's role in <u>Gilda</u>.

This process works equally well in reverse. We can imagine our favorite present-day films recast with actors from a bygone era. Imagine Fred Astaire and Ginger Rogers – or James Cagney and

Judy Garland as the star-crossed lovers in <u>La La Land</u>. Imagine Clark Gable jetting into the future to play Tony Stark and Iron Man in the Marvel Studios superhero blockbuster series. This is a terrific exercise for film appreciation students, and will demonstrate your ability to think critically and outside the box. It is the type of creative thinking and critical analysis that is sure to set your essays apart and capture the attention of your college professors.

Remember, too, that acting (and actor casting) is just one category we may choose to evaluate. Personally, however, it's the area in which I'm most experienced – and, therefore, most comfortable in reviewing. By comparison, I've never had a very good ear for music. When listening to a musical score, for example, it's difficult for me to identify the specific instruments playing – and determine how each one enhances the overall composition. In an essay, then, music would be far more challenging for me to evaluate as a contributing element in a film. Despite this limitation, I can still consider – and write about – music from the most basic and elementary perspective possible. I can pose simple questions like these:

- During which scenes in the film is the music most powerful?

- Can I identify scenes in which the music doesn't quite work?
- Are there any parts of the film in which the music feels overpowering –or distracts attention from the story?
- Is there a point at which the music changes?
- How does this music complement or enhance the action on-screen?
- How does this music affect me emotionally?
- Does the music remind me of the music in any other favorite film?

These are questions that will allow the college writer to think creatively about the relationship of music to film. Even with a discipline that is not the writer's strong suit, asking very basic questions like these provides a clear pathway towards identifying and evaluating key components of a movie's overall success or failure. Therefore, though reviewers are tempted to focus upon our strongest and most familiar areas of film evaluation, we can still train ourselves to delve a little bit deeper into those elements residing slightly outside our comfort zones.

Use the six essays in this book as a guideline, not only in writing essays to review films critically, but also when watching movies purely for entertainment. When viewing films, we have a tendency to relax, sit back, lose ourselves in the overall experience, and enjoy being entertained. Afterwards, it's customary to say: "I liked the movie" or "I didn't." Acquire the habit of asking focused, analytical questions instead. Here are some practical examples to guide you through this new process:

- What do I like most about this film?
- What elements seem to work best?
- Are there any holes in the script?
- Does the dialogue sound natural and realistic – or stiff, stilted, and forced?
- Are there any plot points that remain unresolved by the end of the film?
- How good (or bad) is the acting?
- Do the actors add or detract from the film in specific, measurable ways?
- Who might be a better casting choice in one of the lead (or supporting) roles?
- Can I think of an actor from another time period who would have been brilliant in this role?
- Does the music enhance the story?

- Does the choice of music match the genre of the film?
- Is the lighting of this film remarkable in a specific or unusual way?
- Does the lighting of this film affect me emotionally?
- Is the cinematography reminiscent of other films I've seen?
- Does the style of cinematography evoke a sentiment or emotion I can describe?
- Can I evaluate the sense of movement (or stillness) throughout the film?
- Does this film put forth a certain ideological message?
- How does this film reflect the times in which it was created?
- Will this movie hold up over time, remaining relevant in years to come?
- Does this film represent its genre well?
- Has there been a similar film in recent memory that tells this same story more effectively?
- Does this film do something in a new or different way than we've seen previously?

- Is this film predictable?
- Would I want to watch this film a second time?
- Can I imagine an alternate ending for this film?

I hope these questions will help you begin to watch and study films in specific, measurable ways. I hope this collection of essays will introduce you to a new film or two, as well, and encourage you to think in a more nontraditional manner regarding your viewing and appreciation of films (and television) in general. You may even choose to undertake further study on films and directors that never resonated with you in the past. In time, these can evolve into new stylistic favorites. When you discover a new favorite film, try challenging yourself to examine similar films in the same genre, as well as additional films helmed by the same director.

Throughout the six essays in this book, we will cite several definitive academic textbooks on film. Louis Gianetti's <u>Understanding Movies</u> is an especially good reference volume and a logical place to start. Gianetti's work is comprehensive in scope, and highly detailed in its analysis of motion pictures. More importantly, this is the book most often assigned for film study classes at both the graduate and undergraduate level. Thomas C. Foster's <u>Reading the Silver Screen</u> and David A. Cook's <u>A History of Narrative Film</u> are fine supplementary texts, as well. Remember that sources and references must always be accurately cited in academic writing. Use the references indicated in these six essays, then, as guidelines for citing and supporting your own essay assignments.

Ultimately, I hope the examples in this book will prove helpful when planning and writing college essays for film classes. I hope you will find ways to apply these methods of study and analysis to all your coursework in film appreciation, communications, and the humanities. I hope you will make the most of every academic opportunity that comes your way – and make the most of yourself, as well. Most of all, I hope you will use every ounce of your talent, intelligence, and creativity in every assignment throughout your college, university, and professional careers – and learn to put everything you have into everything you do.

Mike Kimmel
Los Angeles, California

A Note on Style

It's customary in informal writing and print journalism – including film reviews – to list titles of books and movies in italics. This is a familiar and convenient device to set these titles apart from the rest of the narrative text.

However, in academic research papers and manuscripts intended for publication, book and film titles should instead be underlined. This ensures greater clarity and accuracy for purposes of editing, grading, typesetting, and reproduction. In academia, underlining also identifies titles as independently produced projects – not pieces created as components of separate and larger works.

Therefore, for the purposes of this book, film and book titles are underlined. This reinforces best academic standards for students and overall consistency with college coursework. Additionally, when words, phrases, or topics requiring definition or clarification are first introduced, they are underlined, rather than italicized. This, too, is most consistent with MLA essay format.

Genius Acting and Directing in <u>The Gold Rush</u>

Charles Chaplin, writer, director, composer, and star of <u>The Gold Rush</u>, opens the film with a bird's eye view of lonely gold prospectors lugging ponderous equipment up a frozen mountain trail. This setting and opening shot serve an important function. They provide the audience with a unique perspective on the men's infinitesimal size, as contrasted with the awesome vastness of the Yukon territory they hope to conquer.

This difference is accentuated with the introduction of The Little Fellow, as Chaplin preferred to call his character. When we see the familiar figure of Chaplin hiking the terrible trail, our first impulse is to chuckle at how completely out of place he appears. The baggy trousers, tight jacket, giant shoes, and curiously formal hat are completely inappropriate for this locale. The garments appear to offer The Little Fellow minimal protection from the raging elements. Charlie looks to be half the size of the other prospectors, as well. The Little Fellow's appearance contrasts well with the formidable landscape, and sets the stage for an effective "man versus the elements" showdown.

In this opening sequence, director Chaplin employs the technique of <u>mise en scene</u>, the careful framing of visual elements within the shot, to draw attention to his lead character's slender, fragile figure against the mammoth landscape. The Little Fellow and the other prospectors are also placed below the horizon level in the camera frame, emphasizing the dominance of the mountains over the men.

Chaplin utilizes mise en scene effectively later in the film, as well, when The Little Fellow visits the dance hall for the first time. His small body, centered and framed slightly low in the foreground of the massive dance hall powerfully illustrates his character's helplessness and vulnerability in this overwhelming and dangerous locale.

Moreover, the riotous activity of the patrons throughout the dance hall – including those framed above in an upper balcony – lead viewers to despair of The Little Fellow's opportunities for success and mere survival here. We watch him steal a drink from a waiter's tray, revealing subtly that he doesn't have enough money to feed and care for himself. His clothing and diminutive size set him apart from the other revelers, as well, making him an object of ridicule.

He only meets beautiful dance hall girl, Georgia, when she selects him to make another man jealous. Georgia picks our hero out of the crowd as the most unlikely and unimpressive dance partner she can find – hardly an auspicious beginning for The Little Fellow's first venture into Alaska's rugged society. These are all terrific touches of detail crafted by an imaginative film director.

Chaplin establishes setting and changes location effectively through the <u>iris technique</u>, a highly visual means of opening and closing his camera lens with an expanding or contracting dark circle, thus mirroring the function of the human iris. Though Chaplin chooses to open his film with this device, he is careful to use it sparingly. Clearly, the maestro realized, even in 1925, that early film directors were already overusing this popular method.

In his book <u>Understanding Movies</u>, Louis Giannetti references the dual nature of Chaplin's work in film with a thought-provoking quote from the master himself. "Film acting," Chaplin explains, "is unquestionably a director's medium" (246). Nevertheless, Chaplin the actor imbues Chaplin the director with extraordinary sensitivity to the actor's craft. Director Chaplin allows his fellow thespians ample opportunity to ply their craft in revealing close-ups.

Mainstream audiences of today tend to be under-impressed with "old movies," particularly those of the silent film era. Since stars of the silent screen could not use vocal techniques to enhance performance, many of these actors came to rely more heavily upon their physicality. The results were often performances that would today be labeled "over the top," and far better suited for stage than screen. In this respect, <u>The Gold Rush</u> appears to be an early anomaly, and a film well ahead of its time. Chaplin and his cast of silent players are surprisingly "real," delivering performances rich in texture, emotional variety, and pathos throughout this epic production.

Chaplin's own nuances in acting technique are enviable even by today's standards. His minimalist skills are pure genius in scenes that show him eating first a candle, and later his own boot. In close-up, Chaplin's internal moments of discovery help viewers to imagine the pangs of hunger that could drive a civilized human being to feast willingly upon such vile offerings. Chaplin makes the most of his footgear, savoring each nail as if it was a juicy chicken bone. He even offers up a final nail to Big Jim, pantomiming a wishbone pull with the larger man.

Georgia Hale is delightful in close-up, as well, especially in scenes where she begins to realize that The Little Fellow is in love with her. Hale is a master of subtext and internal dialogue. She subtly communicates a cynicism and world-weariness that are well suited to her role as a dance hall girl. Hale's mannerisms and body language paint an eloquent picture of Georgia as a lost and disenchanted young woman – one who might be more comfortable on Fifth Avenue or Sunset Boulevard than in frozen Alaska. Moreover, she seems not to fit in well with the other dance hall girls, leading the audience to wonder just how this smart, sassy, urbane beauty ended up in the middle of icy nowhere. When Georgia accidentally finds her own photo (and the flower Chaplin's character offered her) in his cabin, the audience sees her tough heart begin to melt.

Bearish Mack Swain is also sensational as Big Jim. Swain effectively shows his acting chops when starvation and cabin fever cause his character to hallucinate The Little Fellow transformed into a giant chicken. Swain looks genuinely demented when chasing our hero around the cabin. Later in the film, Swain has a beautiful moment, rising from unconsciousness after being left for dead in the snow by the villain Black Larsen. Swain is absolutely riveting as he walks straight towards camera with the glazed eyes of an amnesiac.

In a supporting role, Tom Murray is quite convincing as the villainous Larsen. Murray is stoic and menacing when we see him alone, burning the wanted poster that bears his own scowling image. The cold, faraway look in his smoldering eyes encourages the audience to speculate on the nature of the crimes that led him to seek sanctuary deep in this frozen wilderness. Murray – a solid and dependable villain of the silent film era – is supremely adept here at conveying the heart and soul of a killer.

The skills, nuances, and internal dialogue displayed by the talented actors of The Gold Rush compare favorably with the work of screen and television stars of today. Moreover, these actors of 1925 were accomplished physical comedians, exhibiting marvelous acrobatic skills to enhance plot points in the story. Chaplin himself performs an astonishing victory dance in his cabin when Georgia accepts his New Year's Eve invitation. He performs handstands and bounces around the room with the energy and pliability of a modern day aerobics instructor. Today's thespians might be taken aback when considering the rigors of performing in the silent film era – and the strength, endurance, and flexibility necessary for its star players to avoid injury and maintain successful, long-term careers.

Our first glimpse of Chaplin's great physical aptitude comes early in the film when Black Larsen orders The Little Fellow out of his cabin. When Larsen opens the door, the blistering wind charges in, pushing the smaller man back. As The Little Fellow struggles forward, the wind continues to push him back in a display of sheer balletic brilliance.

Perhaps the most famous scene of the film is the dinner roll dance Chaplin performs, pantomiming a pair of elegant dancing legs with two rolls and forks. This scene shows Chaplin at his creative best, and serves as a sweet and effective counterbalance to the danger and violence that pervades much of the film. Furthermore, the tiny, delicate nature of the utensils and dinner rolls contrasts powerfully with the looming size of the icy mountains outside the cabin.

With its panoramic sets and majestic outdoor locations, The Gold Rush was, in fact, the longest, most ambitious, and most expensive project Chaplin had ever attempted. Moreover, as Joe Franklin, the longtime TV talk show host, reveals in his fine book, Classics of the Silent Screen, this film "was probably the longest and costliest comedy anybody had made up to that time" (66). Despite the additional pressures this placed on its director and star, The Gold Rush succeeds not only as a comedy – but as a poignant and touching drama, as well. The film also holds up beautifully nearly a century after its release.

Most importantly, Chaplin and his able cast of actors demonstrate the rare ability to combine laughs and thrills within the very same scene. In one of the film's more dynamic early scenes, Big Jim and Black Larson battle it out for control of a gun. Round and round the two beefy men twirl inside the tiny cabin, grappling in a circle. They move clockwise, then counterclockwise, then clockwise again. All the while, the gun points menacingly at The Little Fellow, who struggles in vain to evade its deadly barrel. No matter where Charlie scurries, the gun seems always to find him! The real genius of this scene rests in director Chaplin's ability to create dramatic tension with the two combatants, while still maintaining the brilliant comedic elements audiences have come to expect with all his films.

The Gold Rush – and all Chaplin's films – hold up beautifully with the passing of the decades. Cinema, of course, when compared with literature, painting, sculpture, music, and other popular art forms, is a relatively new medium of expression and communication. Only recently has its history passed the hundred-year mark. Throughout this brief timeframe, many directors have been known for their strong sense of drama, while others have established reputations based upon their comedic gifts. Even today, it is a rare filmmaker who can excel in both distinct areas.

Chaplin, however, could score points in both styles within the framework of the very same scene. He was genius enough to stage scenes with the remarkable complexity of the "Big Jim-Black Larsen gun battle" regularly throughout his career. This unique ability surely contributes to the lasting appeal of <u>The Gold Rush</u>, a particular standout among all the maestro's endearing and enduring works. Chaplin's epic body of work as a director is even more impressive as we consider that filmmakers of his era were still experimenting with the new technology and learning their craft. Unlike his peers, however, Chaplin, while developing his own skills as a director in this new medium, was simultaneously performing on-screen as the number one movie star and top box office attraction in the world.

Ideology in von Sternberg's <u>Blonde Venus</u>

Director Josef von Sternberg opens <u>Blonde Venus</u> with a long trek of American students hiking through Germany's Black Forest. This makes for an unusual beginning to an equally unusual film. Further, the international travel of the idealistic students serves as a subtle foreshadowing of our title character's personal journey as the 1932 film unfolds.

Both the taxi driver and the bevy of German bathing beauties encountered clash sharply with Ned and his traveling companions. The cultural differences between the Americans and Germans are briefly but powerfully communicated in this opening scene, and foretell volumes of the difficulties Ned and Helen must confront after they marry. The American men are funny, charming, and charismatic despite the travails of their long journey. The German women, in contrast, are reclusive and cold. Though they are professional stage performers, they seem surprisingly bereft of interpersonal skills. They keep to themselves, and could not be less interested in this batch of stranded, energetic Yanks.

The storyline is powerful and complex, dealing with sexual politics and the shifting role of women in the workplace. When Ned becomes ill, and the couple is hard pressed for funds, he balks at Helen's offer to return to show business. Ned rages, "It's out of the question! I won't have you go back to the stage!" – as if there were something inherently tainted or immoral in a theatrical career. Moreover, since Helen had a successful stage career when they met, Ned may here be seen as both a stubborn and shortsighted spouse.

The film puts forth a conservative rather than liberal agenda in that Helen battles to hold the family together through her individual efforts, without seeking assistance from society or extended family. Helen is nurturing towards her husband and son, and makes courageous, self-sacrificing choices throughout the film on behalf of her family. Dietrich's Helen is reserved and maintains a regal bearing through her many challenges, silently determining to become the household breadwinner.

As Giannetti explains in Understanding Movies, conservatives in the world "regard the family as a sanctified institution, and anything that threatens the family is viewed with hostility" (427). Dietrich's Helen is a powerhouse example of this ideology. Her icy Germanic manner is perfectly suited to the role of woe-begotten savior. Dietrich is an exceptional actress and a fine casting choice in this role. Whenever she interacts with her young son Johnny, the ice melts beautifully. Dietrich is mesmerizing and enchanting when singing her boy lullabies of her faraway homeland.

Throughout the film, Helen never even raises her voice. Her soulful eyes, however, betray the hurt and sadness she feels when the battle she has undertaken finally becomes too much for her. This is particularly true when the talent agent brandishes his show biz slickness with her in his office. He gets nowhere with our heroine. In her eyes, he is merely a necessary cog in the machine she builds to keep her husband alive and her family intact. Though he never *overtly* chases her around his desk, we get the sense that, if he did, Helen would snap him in half.

In the same way, Helen is proud and fearless when telling a coffee shop manager that she cannot pay an eighty-five cent check for her son's meal. She's forced to do the dishes, but her eyes reveal a calm resignation to comply with anything the manager might have asked of her. Helen will allow nothing to interfere with the success of her mission – not even the destruction of her own soul and reputation. She is a blazing example of self-sacrifice.

As Giannetti elaborates, "An added complication of any ideological analysis involves period and historical context" (430). This is certainly true with <u>Blonde Venus</u>, and can be applied equally well to all our favorite films – both past and present. Like every artistic enterprise, <u>Blonde Venus</u> is a product of the times in which it was created. Women won the right to vote in the United States in 1920. In 1932, when the film premiered, women were still struggling to carve out their place in society and find balance in their lives as workers, wives, mothers, and daughters.

Furthermore, good storytelling – in every film era – allows its viewers to learn something about themselves through the gradual unfolding of the plot and events onscreen. As Francis Ford Coppola explains in his groundbreaking book <u>Live Cinema</u>, "Audiences want themselves and their lives explained and illuminated" (7).

Helen's series of challenges when striking out on her own are considerable – and can still resonate powerfully with single mothers of today. The many obstacles she encounters throughout <u>Blonde Venus</u> indicate von Sternberg and Paramount's intent to remind us that women of the day were still light-years away from achieving equality in the workplace and home. There were many stumbling blocks for females to overcome in

1932 – even with their brand new voter registration cards in hand.

Chief among Helen's obstacles, we might say, is millionaire Nick Townsend, played with suave brilliance by Cary Grant. Grant's handsome countenance is riveting on camera, and the inner dialogue von Sternberg reveals in close-up paints a picture of Nick as both a generous and highly complex man. Though he is described as a rich politician "who runs this side of town," we are shown nothing of his political work and machinations. In fact, he seems to spend all his nights painting the town, and it's difficult to imagine him strolling into his office in the early morning. Viewers may even wonder about his sense of responsibility to the citizens who placed him in that office.

Grant's Townsend, with his tuxedo and top hat, capably represents the dashing, worldly, devil-may-care men who roared their way through the 1920s. Today, with a century of perspective to guide us, we may feel a sense of impending doom each time Nick appears on screen. We know, unfortunately, that he and his bar-hopping brethren are soon to be crushed under the weight of the looming depression and world war.

Grant's legendary looks and charm, together with his character's wealth and power, complicate this storyline nicely, establishing a moral dilemma of epic proportions for struggling Helen. What woman could resist the youthful Cary Grant fawning over her, throwing money around, and begging to take care of her and her son? Perhaps this is the filmmakers' way of justifying Helen's infidelity – by giving her a temptation impossible for any woman to resist. On the very first night they meet, in fact, Townsend writes her a three hundred dollar check – quite a hefty sum in 1932. Coincidentally, this is precisely the amount Helen needs to send Ned off to Europe to begin his medical treatment, a vital plot point in Blonde Venus.

Throughout the film, director von Sternberg emerges as a storytelling genius. He employs a brilliant, underutilized device to flesh out details of the courtship and marriage of Helen and Ned. In the film's early moments, his camera transitions from a close-up of one of the German bathing beauties to a shot of little Johnny kicking in his bathtub. When Helen tucks the boy in, he requests the bedtime story of his parents' meeting. Von Sternberg thus brings his audience up to speed with the story of Helen and Ned's romance in a subtle and highly creative manner.

Despite these clever devices, Blonde Venus is ripe with implausibility. For instance, in the film's most famous scene, Dietrich performs a steamy nightclub song in a gorilla costume. She removes the head and throws her hair back in sultry fashion. Visually, the scene is stunning – particularly on the large screen – in spite of the fact that the concept is preposterous. Marlene Dietrich, with her giant blonde wig and razor-sharp Nordic features, is about as out of place as a performer could be in an African setting. In his fine book, <u>A History of Narrative Film</u>, cinema historian David A. Cook also describes this scene as "the most outrageous variation upon the 'beauty and the beast' metaphor in the history of modern culture" (258).

Moreover, the idea that Helen returns to the stage after a five or six year absence (and after having a child), then rises quickly to the top of the heap in the brutally competitive world of show business is ludicrous, as well. Similarly, it is hard to believe that a man with Nick Townsend's opportunities in life falls so quickly and completely for Helen that he writes her checks on the first night they meet. Despite Helen's exotic beauty and charm, Nick could surely find younger, less encumbered, more willing starlets to woo. Her rapid success on stage is all a bit too convenient – as though von Sternberg wishes to raise Helen up impossibly high and impossibly fast to better dramatize her eventual hard fall.

Later in the film, we see Helen hit rock bottom when she solicits a seedy detective for prostitution. Though it was clearly implied earlier, von

Sternberg now hits us over the head with the realization that Helen has become a streetwalker. The most powerful line of dialogue in the film is delivered when the detective asks Helen if he's hurt her feelings. She replies unemotionally, "I haven't got any anymore." It is at this point that she finally makes the decision to stop running from the law and give up her son.

When we see Helen's nightclub act in Paris, she is an entirely different woman. Her mannish costume, and the flirtatious caress she offers a female dancer, indicate she has now taken a strong turn towards lesbianism. While today's films, of course, are far more explicit, this scene in <u>Blonde Venus</u> was rather blatant for 1932, and must have been quite shocking for American audiences, in particular.

Giannetti reveals in his backstory on Dietrich that she was an openly bisexual actress "when she first arrived in Hollywood, but filmmakers often exploited her ambiguous sexuality with great success" (445). This is mirrored by the fact that Helen fails to swoon when reunited with handsome Grant's Nick Townsend, who still desires her madly. Helen, however, is stronger in Paris and more self-assured. She has risen to the top of the Paris nightclub world through her own efforts and skill – and perhaps with a little help from her newfound sexual identity.

Helen's rise and descent is remarkably quick, spanning only several months. Ned calls her a "princess" prior to her unfortunate series of missteps, dramatically emphasizing the *extent* of her descent into ruin. It is only when the fallen princess returns home, asking meekly to stay, that she is rescued. Townsend, with his wealth and power, did not save her. As the star attraction of the Paris nightclubs, Helen certainly had plenty of money and influence of her own. Townsend, however, does prove to be the catalyst for her return to America and the visit to Ned and Johnny that ultimately reunites the family. Nevertheless, Helen quickly discards the handsome millionaire when Ned agrees to takes her back.

Giannetti hits the nail squarely when discussing women and feminism in the early days of film. The author identifies an unfortunate truth for female characters. He states: "Their main function was to support their men, seldom to lead a fulfilling life of their own. Marriage and a family were their most frequent goals, rarely a meaningful career." (438). Blonde Venus clearly fulfills these parameters and expectations of the day for its filmmakers and studio.

The ideological implication von Sternberg, screenwriters Jules Furthman and S.K. Lauren, and Paramount Pictures put forth throughout this drama is unmistakable: women left unsupervised by their male protectors fall quickly from grace. It is only when they slink back to the home and hearth, with heads bowed and tails tucked, that they are allowed to return to the pedestals upon which their men place them. And if they behave themselves, their husbands might even allow them out of the house every four years to vote.

Anatomy of a Masterpiece: Casablanca

Casablanca, directed by Michael Curtiz in 1942, benefits from an outstanding story and script, a fine place to begin discussion on the film classic. Warner Brothers Studios in Burbank, California houses a tiny museum on the lot that features an engaging display of props and written materials from the film. Perhaps most enlightening of all is a series of scathing telegrams written by mogul Jack Warner to the Epstein brothers, who received the film's first writing credit. Warner berates the scribes mercilessly for their tardiness in delivering completed pages for approval. He threatens to fire the pair, blackball them, and demand return of advances he paid. Given our sense of perspective with Casablanca, and our knowledge of its revered place in film history, it is somewhat jarring to travel back in time, and witness the utter contempt with which its screenwriters were treated in their heyday.

The story is a powerful one, centering on Nazi efforts to destroy a resistance leader in unoccupied French Morocco. Complicating the story beautifully is a love triangle between the leader and his wife, Victor and Ilsa Laszlo, and her former beau Rick Blaine. In the back-story, we learn that Ilsa broke Rick's heart years ago. Rick has since become a jaded, cynical, and empty man, largely as a result of this romantic disappointment.

Now, however, he is also a successful café and casino owner, a respected and highly esteemed businessman in shadowy Casablanca. Rick is a mover and shaker here, and the Laszlos are now in his town and at his mercy. He holds the key to Ilsa and her famous husband's survival: stolen letters of transit the couple needs to escape to America. Rick doesn't seem to care about anyone or anything, however. He is not interested in Victor's worthy cause of Nazi resistance, and is certainly not interested in rescuing the beauty who broke his heart and spirit. "I stick my neck out for nobody," he states coldly in the film's early moments. This certainly appears to be Rick's philosophy on life.

The ideology of Casablanca is unabashedly patriotic, heroic, and moralistic. Rick makes an emotionally charged speech at film's end in which he surrenders all hope for personal happiness in favor of serving the needs of the free world. It is a major shift in attitude from the bitter, tough-as-nails curmudgeon he portrays throughout the film. Louis Giannetti, in Understanding Movies, sheds light on the film's ending, explaining, "Americans and their allies were being called on to make personal sacrifices for a higher cause. One critic has suggested that the movie is not a portrait of the way we were, but of the way we wanted to be" (380). More importantly, however, <u>Casablanca</u> challenges us with the idea that when faced with mammoth personal challenges, human beings have the ability to rise to the occasion and become the heroic, selfless, and altruistic citizens we want and need to be.

The ideology put forth in <u>Casablanca</u> is <u>explicit</u>, as defined by Giannetti (413), in that characters verbally espouse the ideals they wish to convey. Rick's famous airport speech is the most obvious example, but other characters in the film behave similarly. Ilsa calls Rick to task for his unwillingness to help Victor, saying, "One woman has hurt you, and you take your revenge on the rest of the world." She slaps him in the face with the realization that he's turned his back on the dire state of world affairs, whereas he was far more conscientious when she first knew him in Paris. When Victor tells Rick at film's end, "Welcome back to the fight," he appears to symbolize Europe itself, shaking the hand of America for its tardy but much appreciated entry into World War II.

<u>Casablanca</u>'s ideology also reveals itself in a brief but interesting scene Carl shares with an

elderly couple bound for a new start in America. The couple positively glows with hopefulness and the promise of a new life in the States. Throughout the film, in fact, when characters speak of America, they do so reverentially. For the downtrodden masses of the planet, America represents the promise of all the freedoms that are being systematically stripped away by the growing world menace. In outdoor scenes, characters speak of America in hushed tones as they gaze skyward towards the airplanes delivering escape for the fortunate few. The effect, however, is pure directorial genius. These characters actually appear to look up towards heaven and the angels – such is the awe and veneration with which they yearn for America, the great sanctuary of the world. The film's ideology is communicated beautifully and with painstaking care in these engaging and highly evocative visual moments.

A particularly effective story device in <u>Casablanca</u> is the early scene between Bogart's Rick and Señor Ugarte, played with evil gusto by the incomparable Peter Lorre. Despite our knowledge of the great power and influence this film has held for over seventy years, it may be helpful today to imagine the experiences of first-time viewers in the year <u>Casablanca</u> debuted.

Sitting in a darkened theatre in 1942, moviegoers might have anticipated further, deeper, ever more conspiratorial scenes between Bogart, the supreme movie star and Lorre, the undisputed master of film creepiness. However, when viewers see Lorre dragged off by authorities, and learn he's been killed in prison, they're jolted into the realization that anything is possible as this story unfolds. The filmmakers throw their audience an effective psychological curveball here. If Lorre is dispatched so early in the story, then all bets are clearly off. Anything can happen next, and the audience thus learns to hang onto their seats for a thrilling and unpredictable ride. Casting plays a vital role here. A lesser-known character actor in the small role of Ugarte could not have delivered the same punch with an early demise. Lorre's star power accomplishes this effect exceptionally well.

The surprise of Ugarte's early murder serves another important function: to foreshadow and accentuate the tense ending of the film. Up until the very end, when the plane taxis on the runway, we are never really sure what the finale will be. Will Ilsa leave with Rick or Victor? Will she stay behind with Rick? We never know for sure. We can make educated guesses in several directions, and in each case we would be correct. Ingrid Bergman's Ilsa is a bit of a mystery to us, as well. Moreover, she is beautiful enough to make even the most sensible of men behave erratically. Imagine how much lovelier still she must have seemed in the midst of all the chaos, squalor, and corruption of war-torn Casablanca in 1942.

Realistically, Ilsa appears just as likely to choose true love over matrimonial duty. Similarly, Rick is just as capable of shooting Victor as saving him. When Rick holds the gun first on his friend Captain Renault, and then Major Strasser, we get the sense that he's been down this road before – and that he will not hesitate to kill. The storyline of <u>Casablanca</u> keeps us off-balance up until its memorable and poignant conclusion.

The screenplay itself is a beautiful example of taut, skillful writing. Humor and pathos are employed successfully throughout with terse, snappy dialogue. Comedic passages in <u>Casablanca</u> serve as effective counterpoints to the tenseness of the drama and the pervasive sense of oppressiveness and physical danger.

Rick speaks some of the best comic lines in an early scene with the newly arrived German officers. In the following passage, Rick demonstrates a devil-may-care attitude when questioned by the dour Major Strasser. Strasser could probably have Rick shot for his insolence. Rick doesn't seem overly concerned. He deflects the German officer's attempt to discern his political loyalties as follows:

> **STRASSER**
> What is your nationality?

> **RICK**
> I'm a drunkard.

Later, when the Nazi commander baits him with the challenge of a German invasion of America – and specifically New York – Rick fearlessly picks up the gauntlet:

> **RICK**
> There are certain sections of New York, Major, that I wouldn't suggest you try to invade.

The use of sharp, sarcastic dialogue in the script fleshes out the character of Rick. We see Rick Blaine as rough-edged, a mystery man with an uncertain past. We know he's been in tough spots before. Even the calculating Major Strasser, when reading aloud his prepared dossier on Rick's life and background, discovers no clear reason why Rick has landed in this abominable corner of the world. How did he get here? Why is he forced to stay? Captain Renault would like to know the answer as well, but even this close confidante has no definite answer, as evidenced with the following exchange:

> **RICK**
> I came to Casablanca for the waters.

> RENAULT
> Waters? What waters? We're in the desert.
>
> RICK
> I was misinformed.

When Ilsa points a gun at him, Rick voices the most powerful and chilling lines of dialogue in the film.

> RICK
> Go ahead and shoot. I'll make it easier for you. You'll be doing me a favor.

This passage offers us a glimpse of the desperation and pain in which Rick lives his life daily. The script shows us that Rick is truly one of the walking wounded. Though Rick is given most of the best dialogue in the script, Claude Rains' Captain Renault delivers a particularly memorable laugh later in the film, as well:

> RENAULT
> I am shocked, shocked to learn there is gambling here.
>
> EMIL
> Your winnings, sir.

The brilliant script is accentuated by an imaginative use of movement. The action generally moves slowly and deliberately, contributing to a highly charged sense of danger all through the film. This is particularly evident in close-up, with characters carrying on secret conversations and attempting to hide them from prying eyes and ears. When Ilsa and Victor first arrive at Rick's, for instance, they pretend to be interested in a ring for sale. This is a pretext for obtaining information on local resistance efforts from the seller, a freedom fighter. The stillness of the actors and their soft speech draws viewers into the scene, so that we seem to share the peril experienced by its characters. Strong, internalized acting enhances the effect, as Victor, Ilsa, and the partisan communicate beautifully with their eyes.

In contrast, the capture of Señor Ugarte is kinetic and chaotic. Peter Lorre's Ugarte struggles mightily to resist the policemen who haul him away. Another clever directorial touch here is the casting of tall, physically imposing actors to portray the arresting officers. The size of these performers contrasts well with Peter Lorre's relatively modest stature, and imparts an air of fatalism and inevitability as they drag him kicking and screaming to his fate.

With regard to the acting, the cast of <u>Casablanca</u> is arguably one of the strongest ever assembled for a motion picture. Lead players Humphrey Bogart and Ingrid Bergman are exemplary actors who mesmerize us with their technique and shine in every scene together. It is nearly impossible to take our eyes off the two stars, such is their tremendous chemistry together. Never do we believe that these two actors are even remotely distinct from the star-crossed lovers into whose bodies they breathe life on screen. Both are masters of subtlety, and highly gifted in communicating emotion through their eyes.

For Bogart in particular, however, Rick represents the Holy Grail for actors. This is clearly his role of a lifetime. Bogart excelled throughout his career in playing fast-talking, hard-boiled toughs, most notably detectives and criminals. His role in Casablanca, however, offers him opportunity to explore a far greater range and depth of emotion. With his portrayal of Rick, Bogart succeeds in revealing the intense melancholy and vulnerability for which he will forever be remembered.

As an actor, Bogart uses subtle, specific movements and gestures throughout Casablanca. For example, when Ugarte is arrested after a shootout at the cafe, Bogart's Rick takes back control of the situation slowly and masterfully. Rick walks calmly across the floor and speaks to soothe his customers. As he does so, he strolls past a table, reaches down and nonchalantly rights a glass knocked over in the excitement. The action is easily missed, almost imperceptible, as if Rick is in the habit of solving problems unconsciously and by rote. It is an exceptional tiny moment that helps define Rick's character.

In a more obvious example, Rick throws himself into the middle of a fistfight between a German and French soldier, separating the pair roughly. He shows himself here to be a physically formidable man, despite his slender build. Bogart's Rick is no mere back office manager in a spiffy white dinner jacket. He looks perfectly willing to take the jacket off and "step outside" when the need arises. With these brilliant details, Bogart fleshes out the character of Rick as a strong, capable, and energetic leader of men.

Ingrid Bergman is somewhat ahead of her time with her lush portrayal of Ilsa. Bergman's Ilsa is upscale and ladylike, and we get the sense that she could never willingly carry on with two men at the same time. She is thoroughly uncomfortable with the romantic triangle and the reappearance of her one true great love. Nevertheless, we can see that she is nobody's damsel in distress.

Bergman's Ilsa displays great strength of character in flashback. When a friend informs her that Victor is alive and has escaped the concentration camp, she abandons Rick in a manner that breaks his heart – but ultimately guarantees his safety from the German army rapidly advancing on

Paris. Bergman plays her last scene in Paris masterfully. Though she agrees to meet Rick at the train station, we can see the painful secret she holds in her wonderfully expressive eyes. She deceives Rick here to save his life.

When Ilsa arrives in Casablanca, Bergman imbues her with a regal bearing that belies the discomfiture she clearly feels. She is torn between Rick, the love of her life, and Victor, a man she deeply cares for and respects. Bergman portrays Ilsa with a strong bond of spousal fidelity to Victor. Ilsa also experiences shame and guilt at having unwittingly betrayed her marriage with a Paris love affair – when she thought her noble husband was dead. Bergman plays this myriad of conflicting emotions with skill and grace. Moreover, she displays astonishing strength when she pulls a gun on Rick and threatens to kill him to save Victor and his cause. It is only her great love for Rick that stays her hand. We get the sense that any other man who callously keeps the letters of transit from her would be summarily ventilated.

While Rick's sacrifice at film's end is the stuff of which legends are made, Ilsa sacrifices greatly, as well. She makes a decision to close the door forever on her heart's desire – and continue helping her husband in fulfilling his great mission. She joins Rick in a boldfaced lie on the tarmac. Rick tells Victor what he shared with Ilsa was over long ago. He hopes the fabrication will ensure a long and happy union for the pair. Ilsa goes along with the story solemnly, displaying quiet resolve. Victor, of course, is insightful enough to recognize the lie, but gentlemanly enough to let it pass. Bergman shows all her conflicting feelings at the airport with an emotional range that is extraordinary. She may well be the finest actress of her generation.

Paul Henreid and Claude Rains support Bogart and Bergman well in the major roles of Victor and Captain Renault, respectively. Henreid demonstrates tremendous vocal skill, a resource frequently underutilized by film actors. His deep, resonant voice creates a sense of stature and gravitas that accentuates the reserved power and nobility of Victor. In contrast, Rains offers us a spirited mischievousness that is well suited to the role of the morally ambiguous Prefect of Police. He turns in a bravura performance as the lovably corrupt skirt-chaser Renault.

As earlier discussed, Peter Lorre's star power and dramatic chops deepen the intrigue and complicate the storyline nicely. Lorre excels in portraying villains on screen, and his Ugarte is a memorable addition to this rogue's gallery. Similarly, Conrad Veidt is pure evil as the dangerous Nazi officer Strasser, the role for which he is still best remembered. In real life, ironically, Veidt was a popular German actor who married a Jewish woman and vehemently opposed the Nazis. He fled to England to escape a death sentence when Hitler came to power in 1933. Veidt's intimate knowledge of Nazi cruelty and malevolence is evident in his stern and ominous depiction of Strasser. Even today, it is remarkably easy to hate the man on screen – a fact studio executives understood well in the 1940s. Veidt was rumored, in fact, to have been the original choice to play Dracula before the role finally went to Bela Lugosi.

Louis Giannetti speaks of the use of "camp" and "hammy performances" (450). These are employed sparingly – but to great effect – in Casablanca, particularly with the efforts of terrific character actors Sydney Greenstreet, S.Z. Sakall, and Dooley Wilson. These solid, reliable showmen know how to communicate their characters' intents non-verbally, sometimes with a simple roll of an eye or arch of an eyebrow. The skillful use of their comedic gifts helps keep the audience engaged, and cuts the tension at key moments in the story. Particularly memorable is Sydney Greenstreet's Signor Ferrari swatting flies at the conclusion of his business meetings – first with Rick, and later the Laszlos. He conveys the impression that he swats down human beings just as contemptuously, and with as little remorse.

Casablanca, at a tight one hour and forty-three minutes, benefits from creative directorial and editing choices, as well. Director Michael Curtiz keeps the story moving at a rapid pace, with characters in early scenes providing key information about what is to transpire next. We learn of the murder of the German couriers in the same way the film's characters would – from a radio announcer. This device in the film's opening sequence brings viewers instantly into the story. A pickpocket warns his prosperous mark about the suspect round-up, and mentions casually that a pretty girl will also be obtained for Captain Renault. This helps to paint a picture of Renault before we ever meet him. Similarly, characters discuss Rick and his club before he is introduced to us on screen. In this way, Curtiz allows this complex story to unfold in a naturalistic and easily digestible manner.

When Curtiz gives us our first glimpse of Rick, we see him playing chess alone. This is another small touch of directorial genius. Rick appears as a man lost in thought, a man hopelessly trying to outmaneuver himself. Consequently, he is stumped and checkmated. Curtiz sketches out Rick's character with several other effective choices, as well. Gorgeous Ivonne throws herself at him early in the film, but Rick couldn't care less. When casino dealer Emil tells Rick he's lost 20,000 francs, Rick consoles his employee. Rick replies, "It's all right," and "These things happen all the time." Curtiz shows us in these early exchanges that Rick is unflappable, the ultimate cool cucumber. When Rick rescues a young Bulgarian losing badly at the roulette table, however, Curtiz reveals a sensitive heart beating beneath the stone cold exterior. This scene also serves as an effective foreshadowing device for Rick's dramatic and heartfelt transformation at the film's conclusion.

Curtiz provides brief but informative portraits of other characters, as well. He peoples his film with foreigners in strange garb from all over the globe. Tracking shots through Rick's café intrude upon multiple private scenarios as they play themselves out. We see Arabs, Asians, Europeans, South Americans, and some exotic types difficult to identify. We meet a middle-aged man planning to escape Casablanca by boat. He is reminded twice to bring cash. We meet a woman desperate to sell her diamonds. She is offered a price far lower than expected. Though it pains her greatly, she accepts. With these details, Curtiz thrusts his viewers headlong into the action and drama. He is expert at creating an emotionally rich and dangerous landscape in which his characters struggle to live, breathe, escape, and survive.

Curtiz's characters drink often – generally champagne, cognac, and brandy. These are curiously upscale bar choices. They contrast well with the sense we get of characters scrambling to put together money enough just to survive. Curtiz provides another clever detail in that drinking glasses are frequently knocked over and their contents spilled out. This appears to have a symbolic element, perhaps indicating an emptying out of the life-giving merriment these characters love so much in the few French territories still free from the Nazis' iron grip.

Music adds immeasurably to the overall effect of <u>Casablanca</u>, as well. The film's opening theme imparts a potent sense of danger. Moreover, whenever the Nazis are shown, they are backed with a terrifying and severe operatic score that serves to intensify the sense of menace they deliver throughout the storyline. A beautiful guitarist sings solo in Spanish. Her song is a sad, mournful wail, capturing the pessimism of the times and simultaneously reminding us of the multinational population in this city. Heavenly violin music fills the background when Ilsa tells Rick how she first met and married Victor as a young girl. The effect here is inspiring and ethereal, serving to convey the deep feelings of faith she experienced at meeting the famous and heroic freedom fighter she had heard of all her life.

The film's best remembered use of music, of course, is the scene in which Victor leads the musicians in the French national anthem, drowning out the German group that has taken over Sam's piano. Casablanca's patriotic ideology emerges in powerful fashion here, as well, inspiring the French nationals and all the expatriates to unite against their German invaders. Director Curtiz, in fact, wisely uses the backdrop of this musical confrontation as a major turning point in the film. It is the catalyst that precipitates the closing of Rick's café and the subsequent arrest of Laszlo.

Curtiz uses lighting exceedingly well to enhance story elements. Ingrid Bergman is positively luminous in close-up. When she surprises Rick at his apartment, Curtiz has her dressed all in white, with a delicate white scarf about her head like a halo. Curtiz frames her beautifully in the doorway of the dark apartment. Light floods in behind Ilsa to powerful dramatic effect. The lighting gives her an otherworldly appearance, like a goddess, wistful and angelic.

Elsewhere in the film, lighting is used to cast dramatic shadows over the players' faces, and accentuate all the menace and intrigue of the storyline. Shadows from shutters, blinds, and windowpanes fall across characters' bodies as they peek through windows, ominously suggesting prison bars – another brilliant effect.

With regard to mise en scene, long shots are framed so that actors are often situated in the lower half of the screen. As Giannetti explains, this contributes to a sense that "inhabitants seem overwhelmed from above" (63). Curtiz utilizes exotic architectural elements in this manner to further oppress his characters. These objects are employed creatively to intrude between the players. Arches, columns, and posts seem to cut through the heads of his actors, indicating a threat of imminent and violent death, perhaps by beheading.

"When movie specialists speak of framing a shot," Thomas C. Foster further explains in <u>Reading the Silver Screen</u>, "they mean determining how a shot is composed (167)." Foster elaborates on this principle well, also posing many specific questions for audiences to consider. "Many elements go into that act. What visual elements, precisely, are included or excluded? How near or far are they from the camera; that is, do they fill the frame or is there empty space around them? Are they entirely contained by the frame or is part of them lopped off?" Clearly, director Curtiz has considered these questions well in storyboarding and framing <u>Casablanca</u>'s dynamic shots and sequences. The resulting visual effects contribute – subtly but powerfully – to the unfolding of the film's story and message.

In summary, <u>Casablanca</u> still retains all its filmic brilliance, dramatic tension, and extraordinary emotional intensity more than seventy-five years after its release. The comedic moments, too, work just as well today. Casablanca may realistically be considered the gold standard against which great films of every succeeding generation must be measured. Consider, for example, watching the Academy Awards each year. It would an interesting exercise annually to compare the Best Picture winner to Casablanca. We can ask ourselves objectively how each year's winner will hold up over time when compared against the masterpiece of 1942.

Casablanca, with its epic script, dangerous setting, brilliant cast, flawless acting, genius directing, powerful ideology, luminous photography, creative staging, and inspired music stands alone as the preeminent accomplishment in the history of film. It is hard to imagine there will ever be another motion picture as close to perfection as this one. Any viewer who can sit through a screening of this film unaffected, and with dry eyes, must surely have a heart made of unyielding stone.

Light and Movement in
Taxi Driver

In <u>Taxi Driver</u>, director Martin Scorsese uses movement and light in a variety of imaginative ways to explore the title character's journey through a physically and psychologically dangerous world. Scorsese's creative techniques in this regard impart a surreal effect throughout the film, highlighting the increasing loneliness and alienation of the main character, Travis Bickle, in Paul Schrader's evocative screenplay.

The actual occupation of taxi driver, in fact, serves as a powerful device to indicate Bickle's movement through gritty and dangerous streets. The cab itself is a vehicle hurtling through the crime and grime of New York City's savage and oppressive landscape. With its armored hull and bulletproof partition, the cab protects and insulates Bickle from the endless, sleepless, soulless terrors of the brutal city that appears to keep him hopelessly checkmated.

In a sense, however, Bickle's cab may be viewed as a moving metaphor for his own powerlessness. Scorsese utilizes the taxi as a means of indicating that DeNiro's character is helpless against the numerous overwhelming forces in his life that seem dedicated to his eventual destruction. Despite his efforts towards positive forward movement – and despite his impressive physical abilities and skill behind the wheel of the vehicle – Travis Bickle is clearly a man going nowhere fast. He is thwarted and frustrated at every turn, in every area of life, and is unable to move forward – in spite of the fact that his job keeps him moving continuously.

In the areas of romance and socialization, Travis is astonishingly ill-equipped to compete in the real world. Realistically, Robert DeNiro's Travis Bickle is a nice enough looking twenty-six year old bachelor. However, he is embarrassingly unable to compete with other young men in the dating arena. Moreover, he appears to have no friends, nor even to maintain contact with his family in nearby New Jersey.

It is positively painful to watch Bickle take Betsy (Cybill Shepherd) into a porno theatre on their second date – especially after the somewhat favorable first impression he had earlier made. In two wonderful prior scenes, Travis boldly walks into Betsy's office, introduces himself, and later takes her out on a coffee date. Although beautiful, educated Betsy appears to be far out of Travis' league, she is curiously engaged by the intense, well-mannered, blue-collar oddball. Travis wastes little time in turning her intrigue into revulsion by their second date. So we see that although the taxi driver is able to start the lady's engine, he quickly drives himself off the nearest cliff.

The importance of cinematic movement, in fact, cannot be overemphasized. Thomas C. Foster explains this principle brilliantly and succinctly in his fine book, <u>Reading the Silver Screen</u>. "We never say that we're going to hear a movie," Foster tells us. "I doubt that anyone has ever said that. We watch one. Always. (57)"

Scorsese employs a subtle, yet interesting, example of movement throughout the terrific scene in which Travis struts into Palantine campaign headquarters and introduces himself to Betsy. During their conversation, co-worker Tom – played with twitchy sagacity by the vastly underrated Albert Brooks – paces back and forth several times, spying and eavesdropping on the pair. Tom's nervous movements present an effective counterpoint to Travis and Betsy's calm and stillness during their psychologically dynamic (yet physically static) first conversation.

Scorsese may be employing a foreshadowing device here, as well. Travis and Betsy's hopes for a potential romance – like their physical bodies in this scene – never truly have an opportunity to move forward. The unlucky duo is rooted forever in the immobile potentialities of their hopeful first encounter.

It is not only New York's upwardly mobile females with whom Bickle fails to connect. He strikes out dismally with a candy concession girl at another X-rated theatre early in the film. Simply asking the young lady for her name is enough to make her scream for the manager. Scorsese here uses the darkness and dreariness of the low rent porno house to emphasize Bickle's severe isolation, loneliness, and inability to become close with another human being. These sensations are heightened and given a somewhat ironic twist by their extreme contrast with the background moans of the naked figures frolicking together on the Times Square movie screen.

Although Travis Bickle's taxi cab becomes a means of sustenance for him, it fails to satisfy his needs. In a sense, the cab is a limiting device for Bickle. It moves, but never truly takes him where he wants to go. It is a stroke of pure, dumb luck, in fact, that the car leads Bickle to New York's then rather seedy Union Square neighborhood. Here he crosses paths with an underage prostitute and her abusive pimp. This chance meeting – that takes place in the cab while Travis absentmindedly cruises for fares – effectively seals his fate and places him on the fast track towards his own ruin. In this manner, Scorsese demonstrates that the lead character is never really his own man. Scorsese further shows us here that Bickle is woefully unable to extricate himself from his negative environs, and move himself towards more positive locales and social experiences.

Moreover, the taxi does not even belong to him. It is a company-owned vehicle. In a conversation with fellow cabbie and reluctant guru Wizard (Peter Boyle), we learn that the "fleet has no spares" because the owner is married to a former Miss New Jersey beauty queen. The drivers can thus be seen as hangers-on, hapless employees scrounging for scraps from an unseen employer who effectively pulls their strings. As the newcomer, Travis is the lowest man on this grungy totem pole.

Wizard further divulges that he's never owned his own taxi, either – though he's worked as a driver for twenty years. In this revealing aside, Scorsese demonstrates a bleak potential future for Travis, indicating that our hero may look forward to a lifetime of subservience on the night shift to the stingy, unseen owner. With these fleeting, but highly significant details, Scorsese and screenwriter Paul Schrader effectively paint Bickle into a corner, subtly raising the stakes as the story unfolds while continuing to underscore the young man's helplessness and ineptitude in the face of increasingly dire circumstances.

Even when Bickle starts out upon his regimen of physical training, he proves unable to follow through. Soon after he declares, "no more bad food, no more destroyers of my body" in narration, he is seen guzzling alcohol in another porno theatre! With this disparity, Scorsese and Schrader show us that Bickle's words and intentions are incongruent with his actions. This casual example solidifies the film's underlying assertion that our lead player is never in control of his destiny. With each subsequent failure, he readjusts, setting his sights progressively lower. When Travis fails to assassinate Senator Palantine, he immediately takes aim upon the far less formidable downtown pimps. When he strikes out with Betsy, he opts to become the white knight for damaged, naïve Iris.

The almost constant movement of rain through the film emphasizes the dark, depressed world in which Travis lives. He is battered senseless by the elemental fury of the New York waters. Moreover, whenever the sun *does* come out, it is stark and oppressive, beating all those beneath its rays into submission. This is the same lighting technique Louis Giannetti describes in the 1996 film *johns* (Color Plate 9). It is enough, in fact, to make viewers wonder if New Yorkers *ever* experience fair weather. However, the use of pounding rain and drenching sun help to drive home the message that everything in Travis Bickle's world is decidedly *unfair*. Perhaps the most powerful and prescient line of dialogue is delivered in the film's early minutes, when Travis narrates, "someday a real rain will come and wash all the scum off the street." This, of course, foreshadows his violent turn in the film's conclusion.

There are two interesting scenes in <u>Taxi Driver</u> in which Travis breaks bread with females. The indoor lighting at both casual eateries is severe and overly bright. In the first example, Travis enjoys a coffee date with Cybill Shepherd's Betsy. In the second scene, he buys breakfast for teen prostitute Iris, played brilliantly by Jodie Foster.

In each case, DeNiro's body language is uncomfortable, cramped, and twitchy. Though he tries to exude confidence and composure with both the woman and the girl, he is clearly ill at ease in each situation. His body movements and inner character dialogue function powerfully in conjunction with the strong lighting. The combined effect is that Travis appears overwhelmed by the light – and perhaps by his female companions, as well. Scorsese and director of photography Michael Chapman use lighting and filters here as mechanisms to indicate the young man's severe discomfiture with females. In this respect, they paint a picture of Travis as a nocturnal New York cockroach, toiling efficiently during the midnight hours, but caught defenseless when we turn on the kitchen light. Unlike the roach, however, Bickle doesn't seem to have enough sense to scurry for cover.

Scorsese and Chapman also employ lighting to create the soft, painterly effect Giannetti describes in the 1995 epic Braveheart (23). In this way, the pair transforms the hard lights of New York's nighttime streetscape into fluid, flowing, impressionistic elements behind Travis as he walks and drives through the battlefield city. This painterly effect is enhanced by a liberal use of slow motion throughout the film – and contrasts sharply with the concrete toughness of Travis' life, his body, his background, and his journey.

With respect to the technique of mise en scene, Scorsese frequently places DeNiro near the edge of frame. As Giannetti explains, this tends to reduce the significance of characters thus situated (52-53). In contrast, a character centered in frame, would appear to be "the star of the show." Scorsese employs this strategy particularly well in the "you talking to me?" scene in Bickle's tiny apartment. In the porno theatre with Betsy too, Travis slumps downward and backward in his seat, emphasizing his lower status and anonymity in the world.

One benefit to revisiting a masterpiece like <u>Taxi Driver</u> so many years after its release is our ability to rewind and replay through the magic of first VHS, then DVD, and now digital streaming technology. Today, we can examine the newspaper clippings of Bickle's violent rampage in frame-by-frame detail.

In so doing, we learn that Harvey Keitel's character (called both "Matthew" and "Sport") is actually named Charles *Rain*. This is yet another curious reference to the movement of water, and the idea of washing away all our sins.

Moreover, Paul Schrader reveals in the DVD Collector's Edition ("Taxi Driver Stories" Featurette) that he selected the name "Travis" for its similarity to the word "travel." With this, Schrader intended to convey his title character's doomed, heroic journey. Schrader also created an effective impediment for him with the surname "Bickle," derived from "bicker" – and intended to symbolize the young man's ordinariness and inability to make peace with others (and ultimately himself).

Finally, Travis complains throughout the film of his inability to sleep. Living, working, and slowly going mad in "the city that never sleeps," Travis may ultimately be seen as a microcosm of complex, raging New York itself. Despite all his movement throughout the city, Travis never *travels outside* the confines of New York. Even when Palantine asks Travis in their chance encounter what he'd most like to change about the *nation*, the taxi driver can only respond in terms of his own isolated geography: "whatever they do, they should clean up *this city.*" Manhattan Island might well be seen as a prison colony for Travis – like his own, not-so-private

Alcatraz. Though Travis survives a deadly gunfight in the brothel, it is the teeming, raining, overpopulated metropolis itself, in fact, that finally defeats him and emerges as "winner and still champeen."

In the film's very last scene, we find a somewhat mellowed Travis, now recovered from his hospital stay and driving his taxi once again into the dark, rainy night – like Sisyphus pushing his boulder forever up the hill. For the first time in the film, he appears calm. He seems strangely relaxed, as if he has finally come to accept his station in life. In a too-convenient plot twist, he picks up an unexpected passenger – Betsy, coming out of a hotel at four in the morning. Their final conversation is forced and unnatural, with an impenetrable, bulletproof barrier separating them in the cab. This is one last ironic slap in the face for our humbled hero. Travis is permitted one final look at his unrequited heart's desire before riding off again into the lonely night. Ultimately, then, Scorcese shows us with his last scene that the concrete city has fully ensnared, entombed, and emasculated the troubled young man.

Editing Brilliance in Annie Hall

In Annie Hall, director and lead actor Woody Allen uses a variety of unusual staging and editing techniques in extremely imaginative ways to deliver his manic comedic messages. As a filmmaker, Woody Allen breaks rules and filmic conventions as easily and recklessly as the rest of us break and discard peanut shells at a baseball game. Ultimately, however, Allen succeeds in honoring the single most vital rule of the cinema: to produce a great movie that people truly enjoy, and that withstands the test of time.

The film opens with a sharp, somewhat startling cut from opening credits to a medium shot of Allen speaking directly into camera. Groucho Marx – a longtime influence for Allen – often used this bold technique in the early days of film, most notably in 1937's Horse Feathers. In an apparent homage to the master comedian, Allen actually mentions Groucho in this opening monologue. Speaking into the camera *and* referencing Groucho Marx are strong creative choices by a supremely confident film director. It is essentially the equivalent of Allen planting a flag and staking out a claim on fresh, new comic ground. With this opening piece, he is putting the audience on notice that they are in the hands of a true comedic genius – and perhaps a modern-day successor to Groucho himself.

Another highly inventive editing device is Allen's use of a split screen to demonstrate extreme contrast between scenes and characters. He does this twice to great effect, and slips into each split screen quickly and subtly. Allen employs this technique initially when his own character, Alvy Singer, meets and dines with Annie's oddball family for the very first time. Allen's voice-over narration against a backdrop of chaotic activity drives home the fact that neurotic Alvy feels quite out of place amongst the Halls. Later in the film, Allen revisits the split screen technique to accentuate the differences between Annie's therapy session and his own.

The first example merits further discussion. As a means of illustrating the striking differences between Annie's family and the Singers, Woody splits the screen and shows a mirror image of a family dinner from his youth. A subtle but effective touch here is that Allen's evening meal is dredged up from the 1940s of his childhood, while Annie's family dinner is enacted in then present-day 1977. This adds an additional element of contrast and contradiction to the two family meals.

In a particularly surreal touch, Annie's mother on the left side of the split screen speaks back and forth with Alvy's mother and father on the right. The interaction is a brief one. Allen is genius enough not to hit his audience over the head with this exchange. It happens so quickly, in fact, and with such minimalist skill, that viewers might just chuckle and not fully realize the extremely jarring interaction just witnessed. The three characters have effectively traversed time and space in front of our eyes. Before we have a chance to question out loud what just happened, Allen cuts completely from both dining rooms, and moves the story quickly to his famous "driving in the rain" scene.

Allen bends time and space handily throughout the film. He frequently cuts to flashback sequences of Alvy and his neurotic family while narrating stories from his childhood. This can be rather standard fare in the world of film, as well as television, and even live theatre. Allen throws his audience a curveball, however, when he switches place with his childhood self – an extraordinary editing trick. Schoolboy Alvy walks to the front of his Brooklyn classroom to receive punishment from his teacher. Allen's camera begins to follow the boy – then abruptly cuts back to the rear of the room to discover forty-year old Alvy sitting in his childhood seat and interacting with the youngsters as though there were nothing out of the ordinary about it.

The effect here is both jarring and hilarious. Adult Alvy, sitting in the tiny old-fashioned seat, is thoroughly out of place with the 1940s Brooklyn kids. Still, his earnestness among these children is strangely compelling. This serves to convince us that the successful, adult artist we see on screen is still fighting unresolved battles of thirty years past. With this technique, Woody Allen strikes a resounding psychological chord with his audience. Who among us would not relish the opportunity to go back in time to stand up for ourselves armed with "what we know now?" How wonderful would it be to confront the injustices of childhood armed with our adult knowledge and experience? These are purely rhetorical questions, of course, but they point to an essential strength of Woody Allen's films – the director's ability to build rapport with an audience by identifying common yearnings and exaggerating them to an extreme and absurd degree. In the classroom example, Allen's clever use of editing adds immeasurably to the effect.

Allen uses another smart editing tactic to bend time in his flashback sequences. Louis Giannetti, in <u>Understanding Movies</u>, describes Raymond Spottiswoode's concept of "cutting at the peak of the 'content curve'" (145). Allen, again working subtly, jazzes up the standard film flashback by cutting to the past at the peak of the content curve. For example, when Annie and Alvy walk along the beach and discuss ex-lovers, the action cuts abruptly to flashbacks of each ex-partner whenever their name is mentioned. This keeps the action flowing seamlessly through scenes that are primarily dialogue driven, while simultaneously allowing the audience a peek through the bedroom keyhole.

Allen employs another inventive device early in the film to settle a score with an obnoxious blowhard standing behind him in a movie theatre line. Allen steps out of line, walks straight to camera, and pleads his case directly to the audience. The loudmouth follows Allen, also breaking the fourth wall to speak with us. Allen then struts across frame in a long, tracking shot to deliver philosopher and cultural icon Marshall McLuhan, the subject of their argument. McLuhan neatly puts the offending gent in his place. We might call this a modern spin on the ancient <u>deux ex machina</u> device, with scholarly giant McLuhan stepping in to effectively resolve a crisis and save the intellectual day.

Allen utilizes the technique of <u>jump cut</u> (or <u>smash cut</u>) described in Giannetti's book to powerful effect in the aforementioned dinner scene with Annie's family (136). This technique involves an abrupt, jarring camera movement from one character or scene to the next. Allen delivers a tremendous visual laugh with the jump cut by focusing momentarily on Annie's grandmother, Grammy Hall. In the backstory to this scene, Diane Keaton's Annie speaks unashamedly of her grandmother's virulent anti-Semitism. When we finally meet the matriarch, we clearly see the distrust in her eyes as she scrutinizes Alvy. In another clever bit, Allen juxtaposes his camera to deliver a "Grammy's eye view" of Alvy. A quick, skillful edit reveals Alvy as the grandmother sees him – with a long beard and the stereotypical black hat and garb of a rabbi.

This editing gag may be the best laugh in the entire film. It is totally unexpected, and serves as an effective counterpoint to the intellectual and highly verbose humor for which Allen is best known. It is also reminiscent of the terrific visual jokes employed by the Marx Brothers themselves.

Curiously, Allen stages his action in <u>long shot</u> (i.e. at a far distance) throughout much of the film. Considering his reverence for the inner life and angst of his characters, this is a surprising directorial choice. Director Allen uses long shots frequently when following Alvy and Max, Alvy and Annie, and Alvy alone while interviewing random passersby on the New York streets. In a sense, Allen the director subordinates his role to Allen the screenwriter here in an effort to best advance their collective storyline.

Particularly effective is Allen's use of editing to generate comic/dramatic tension in the aforementioned "driving in the rain" scene. When Annie's creepy brother Duane (Christopher Walken) confides his desire to steer his car into oncoming headlights in the dark, neurotic Alvy is taken aback. Moments later, director Allen pans right to left inside Duane's car to reveal stoic Duane, thoughtful Annie, and frantic Alvy. While this is another solid visual laugh, the scene holds a deeper significance for Alvy. Allen essentially shows his audience that Alvy Singer is incapable of relaxing, and that the odds are hopelessly stacked against him with Annie's family. Even a simple drive to the airport is tortuous for him. With this scene, Allen leads us to expect that Alvy will have similar challenges with all women – and their families – he encounters in the future.

Finally, an enjoyable benefit to revisiting <u>Annie Hall</u> after many years is the opportunity to spot stars of today performing smaller roles early in their careers. These thespians include Beverly D'Angelo, Shelley Duvall, Shelley Hack, Sigourney Weaver, and a very young Jeff Goldblum – who speaks the memorable line, "I forgot my mantra." This reinforces both Allen's skill behind the camera, and his vision in casting so many bit players destined to achieve stardom in the future. Moreover, it indicates Allen's extraordinary ability to create a film that maintains all its original power, charm, and social significance with the passing of the decades. Allen's bold, inventive editing choices throughout <u>Annie Hall</u> work miracles in building an enduring masterpiece with every successive, psychologically taut scene.

Star Wars: The Story is Star

George Lucas single-handedly brought about a resurgence of interest in the science fiction genre with Star Wars, his 1977 critical and commercial success. Lucas assumed both writing and directing duties on the film, thereby ensuring the fulfillment of his artistic vision in bringing script to screen. A pitfall to this approach, of course, is the possibility of acquiring "tunnel vision" with the project, and failing to incorporate different points of view. Fortunately, Lucas' bold ideas and technical skills are more than equal to the challenge. With Star Wars, he has effectively created a new – and convincing – reality that has captured the imagination of movie fans worldwide. Lucas' vision has proven so powerful and enduring that he has continued to keep us all spellbound for more than forty years.

In Understanding Movies, Louis Giannetti explains Aristotle's distinction between mimesis (showing) and diegesis (telling) in the art and craft of storytelling (334). In Star Wars, Lucas leans heavily towards mimesis in that he clearly prefers to keep dialogue to a stark minimum, bringing his mammoth space opera to life visually for the audience instead.

Lucas sets the stage and prepares us for strong visual events in the opening moments of the film. Even with the size and spectacle of the opening title sequence, Lucas establishes a larger than life tone for Star Wars. We are thus instructed to now modify our existing definitions of size and perspective. Next, by putting a dramatic angle on the pursuit of a rebel ship by the massive Empire vessel, Lucas thrusts his viewers headlong into the fray. Both ships seem to pass directly over viewers' heads, showing us their mechanical underbellies, and showing the vessels and their chase frighteningly up close for the audience.

In a sense, then, the storytelling style of Star Wars is intended to be realistic – rather than sanitized or genre-specific, as was the case in the early days of science fiction. The realism of Star Wars, however, is an extremely *heightened* form of realism. Lucas succeeds in convincing us that the events unfolding on screen are both real and logical – in spite of the overpowering presence of otherworldly gadgets, spaceships, and monsters that characterize and define the film's genre.

Star Wars' realism, of course, is tempered by a willing suspension of disbelief amongst viewers. Once we accept the premise that young Luke is a capable amateur pilot prevented by family obligations from joining the academy fleet, it is perfectly reasonable to see him zipping around the galaxy as Obi-Won Kenobi takes him under his wing. We also get an inkling of the unfulfilled dreams of young Luke aching to break loose. Before the final battle sequence, Luke mentions that he "used to bulls-eye womp rats" back home on Tatooine, leading us to believe he can hit the tiny target and deliver a death blow to the Death Star.

Similarly, once we become accustomed to the sight of giant Chewbacca lumbering about, we learn to accept (and expect) that the film will introduce us to a wide variety of strange new species. Some of these will be friends and others foes – just as we've all experienced with our fellow humans. This realization comes to us somewhat unconsciously, and begins to feel rather normal and comfortable as this epic space opera unfolds.

Further, it is a tribute to Lucas' ability to tell the story realistically that we never question how Han Solo communicates so easily with Chewbacca and his unintelligible growls. In the wild Mos Eisley cantina scene, too, Han speaks English with an alien bounty hunter who jabbers on in another incomprehensible space language – just before being blown to smithereens. We've seen similar (but earthly) examples in films before, most notably in

Mike Kimmel

<u>The Godfather</u> and its sequels. In the Coppola films, we barely take notice when one character carries on a conversation in Italian and another responds in English. With this same offhand technique, Lucas pulls us ever deeper into his story, allowing his audience to become increasingly comfortable in these wild, otherworldly settings.

Given our forty years' perspective on the blockbuster film, it is interesting to go back and note the actual sparseness of the dialogue. Lucas takes great pains to keep idle chatter to a minimum, telling his story instead in pictures. For example, when Leia kisses Luke before their perilous rope swing, she says only two words: "For luck." No other mention is made of a spark between the pair – except for a brief exchange in the Millennium Falcon cockpit when Luke indicates disapproval at Han's apparent interest in the Princess.

Even when Obi-Wan instructs Luke in the ways of The Force, he is curiously tight-lipped. Most viewers *want* to hear more, but director Lucas prefers to maintain a sense of mystery throughout the film. In this manner, viewers may "fill in the blanks" for themselves, imagining specific details that are most congruent with their own world views and religious beliefs. This pervasive sense of understatement works effectively to counter-balance the backdrop of giant, explosive spectacle throughout the epic film.

Moreover, Star Wars is essentially free of subplot. There is no real romantic component to the film, save for the slightest hint of a spark Leia shares with both Luke and Han. George Lucas provides only a creeping indication of the relation between Luke and Darth Vader, as well. Whatever story needs to be resolved between them is retained for the sequel film. In this way, Lucas maintains the pristine nature of Star Wars as a simple and incredibly powerful morality play – albeit on a far larger than normal scale.

Interestingly, there is nothing particularly notable about Luke prior to his transformation. He is a rather standard – and somewhat tame – boy next door. We might even go so far as to call Luke a male ingénue. He lines up perfectly with Joseph Campbell's hero prototype in The Power of Myth. In describing classic heroes and their typical quest or journey throughout world mythology, Campbell would classify young Luke as "someone from whom something has been taken, or who feels there's something lacking in the normal experiences available or permitted to the members of his society. This person then takes off on a series of adventures beyond the ordinary, either to recover what has been lost or to discover some life-giving elixir. It's usually a cycle, a going and a returning" (152).

In fact, it is Luke's very ordinariness that helps explain the monumental success of Star Wars in 1977, as well as its lasting appeal through the following decades. We relate more easily to Luke than we would to a more complex and dynamic hero figure – or a larger than life movie star in this same role. A more recognizable young actor of 1977, say Robert Redford, Henry Winkler, or John Travolta, would have been distracting to the storyline as Luke Skywalker. Mark Hamill, with his bright-eyed innocence and everyman charm, is perfect, giving us a more down-to-earth and *accessible* hero.

By casting Hamill in the lead, Lucas effectively delineates the *story* as the film's single most important element. This is a strong contrast to the role casting played in Casablanca – specifically with Peter Lorre's character, Señor Ugarte, who is killed off early in the film despite that actor's major star power. In this respect, Star Wars has much in common with low-budget films in the horror genre, ironically. Horror movies, in general, do not require star name actors in order to be financially successful. These films can therefore – even with their gory special effects – often be produced on very modest budgets.

Similarly, Carrie Fisher's Leia – though charming and charismatic – is a somewhat prototypical

Princess forced into the role of damsel in distress. She is not really much different from Rapunzel or Sleeping Beauty. We may as well call her Snow White on a spaceship. Fisher is a fine actress, and certainly makes her character likable enough on-screen. However, aside from a few edgy remarks to Han and Chewie, Leia doesn't really do much of anything. This is not intended as a criticism of either Lucas or his big-screen creations. Rather, it points to the director's resolve to keep character development to a minimum. Lucas clearly wants nothing to interfere with the unfolding of his epic storyline. <u>Star Wars</u>, then, becomes an essentially star-proof vehicle under Lucas' expert command.

While Alec Guinness lends name recognition to the cast, it is only in the supporting role as Luke's mentor. Besides, his character is killed off relatively early in the film. Remarkably, in fact, despite the film's great commercial success, only Harrison Ford made the leap to superstardom. Mark Hamill and Carrie Fisher's careers never truly soared in the way one might expect – given the astonishing level of exposure they received through this groundbreaking film. The <u>Star Wars</u> *story*, however, proved strong enough to generate a legion of additional blockbuster films, as well as a television series, video games, novels, comic books, and enough toys to make budget-conscious parents weep.

Giannetti also discusses "passive characters – people to whom things are done" and their relation to story (345). The late casting director and acting coach Michael Shurtleff preferred to call these "oh, really characters" – meaning that they only existed in the script to show up and say "oh, really" to the lead players. <u>Star Wars</u> is blissfully free of characters that clutter the action – except perhaps for a couple of rebel military commanders guiding the assault on the Death Star.

Even Luke's aunt and uncle – though seen only briefly – serve an important function early in the film. Their murder by the evil Empire breaks Luke's ties to his home planet and provides him with opportunity and motive to seek out his greater destiny. With this event, Lucas reveals his meticulous attention to detail, as well as his conscientiousness in maintaining the pristine nature of Star Wars as a simple morality play performed on a monumental scale. Lucas shows us that supporting characters – even those with as little screen time as Uncle Owen and Aunt Beru – have been written into the script to move his storyline forward in a substantive manner.

In <u>Myth and the Movies</u>, Stuart Voytilla makes a compelling case that <u>Star Wars</u> precisely follows the mythic, heroic structure illustrated by Joseph Campbell in <u>The Power of Myth</u> and his subsequent works. Luke's adventures mirror Campbell's classic hero's journey, primarily because Luke initially rejects his role as hero. Later, when his familiar life has been destroyed, he makes the conscious choice to follow the hero's path (his call to arms) with the aid of a mentor (Obi-Wan). The teacher then makes the ultimate sacrifice (lowering his weapon in the battle with Vader) to ensure the success of the greater cause (the rebellion) and the completion of the hero's transformation (into a Jedi knight).

Writer/director Lucas has proven to be a capable captain for our hero's journey with his strong commitment to the highly successful framework of mythical story structure. With his groundbreaking masterpiece <u>Star Wars</u>, Lucas takes us all on a thrilling ride out to the furthest reaches of space – and his own extraordinarily vivid imagination and creativity. Even today – with more than four decades of perspective since the epic space opera's release – we see that <u>Star Wars</u> retains every bit of its original grandeur, majesty, and thrilling sense of style and adventure. It is truly an epic for the ages, remaining fully as relevant and watchable today as when it first broke ground – and box-office records – back in 1977.

Afterword

A final – and favorite – idea to consider is the concept of the <u>fish out of water</u> and its relation to principal characters in our favorite films. A fish out of water is a familiar idiom, or figure of speech, used to describe a character thrown headlong into unfamiliar and uncomfortable surroundings. A character in this situation usually faces seemingly insurmountable challenges, as well. The fish out of water technique is an incredibly effective storytelling device, and Hollywood has been capitalizing upon it since the early days of film. This clever theme is nearly always successful, helping filmmakers build exciting, engaging storylines. It works equally well in comedy and drama. It establishes a film's main character as an underdog, encouraging a strong sense of connection and rapport with the audience.

Countless films have used the fish out of water technique effectively, including <u>The Godfather</u>, <u>Rocky</u>, <u>Beverly Hills Cop</u>, <u>The Shawshank Redemption</u>, <u>Big</u>, and – perhaps the most literal example – <u>Splash</u>. In general, title characters in all popular superhero films may also be described as fish out of water characters, thereby enhancing their overall appeal in a subtle but substantive manner. In considering the six films studied in this book, we see that each protagonist fits the fish out of water description, as well. Watch for this underlying theme when viewing films, and you will be surprised at how often – and effectively – it is used.

A Simple Technique for Improving College Essays

Like the films we study, all of us are products of the times and settings into which we were born. As such, we are subject to the standards and conventions of societal behavior and mores. In the Internet age, it's increasingly common for college students to research their essays entirely online. The references listed on college papers, then, now tend to be predominantly electronic. Try your best to resist this temptation in your own essays. Many college professors – particularly those with a little gray in their hair – view a long list of webpage links as "intellectual laziness." Make an effort, therefore, to include several print sources in your bibliography, as well. Even a modest effort in this direction will enable you to stand out boldly from the crowd.

Many excellent references for your essays are not available online simply because they've never been scanned and uploaded. Many of these books are also out of print. A little time spent poring through the dusty old stacks at the library will be invaluable to you. You may discover an old book or two that offers a unique perspective on your essay topic. You'll also show your professors that you don't fit the stereotype of the distracted young student constantly on the phone. Try it. Roll up your sleeves and dive into those old-school library stacks. I predict you'll be very happy with your results – and that your professors will too.

Appendices

Appendices

Works Cited

<u>Annie Hall</u>. Dir. Woody Allen. Columbia, 1976. DVD. Sony, 1999.

<u>Blonde Venus</u>. Dir. Josef von Sternberg. Paramount, 1932. VHS. Universal, 1992.

Campbell, Joseph. <u>The Power of Myth</u>. New York: Anchor, 1991.

<u>Casablanca</u>. Dir. Michael Curtiz. Warner Brothers, 1942. VHS. MGM/UA, 1988.

Cook, David A. <u>A History of Narrative Film</u>. 4th ed. New York: Norton, 2004.

Coppola, Francis Ford. <u>Live Cinema and its Techniques</u>. New York: Liveright, 2017.

Foster, Thomas C. <u>Reading the Silver Screen</u>. New York: Harper, 2016.

Franklin, Joe. <u>Classics of the Silent Screen: A Pictorial Treasury</u>. New York: Citadel, 1959.

Giannetti, Louis. <u>Understanding Movies</u>. 9th ed. Upper Saddle River: Prentice, 2002.

Koch, Howard. <u>Casablanca: The Complete Script and Legend Behind the Film</u>. 2nd ed. New York: Overlook, 1983.

Shurtleff, Michael. <u>Audition: Everything an Actor Needs to Know to Get the Part</u>. New York: Walker, 1978

<u>Star Wars</u>. Dir. George Lucas. Twentieth, 1977. DVD. Twentieth, 2006.

<u>Taxi Driver</u>. Dir. Martin Scorsese. Columbia, 1976. DVD. Sony, 1999.

<u>The Gold Rush</u>. Dir. Charlie Chaplin. United, 1925. DVD. Warner, 2003.

Voytilla, Stuart. <u>Myth and the Movies</u>. New York: Wiese, 1999.

Recommended Reading

Anger, Kenneth. Hollywood Babylon. New York: Dell, 1981.

Blum, Daniel. A Pictorial History of the Silent Screen. New York: Grosset, 1953.

Bonomo, Joe. Strongman: The Daredevil Exploits of the Mightiest Man in the Movies. New York: Bonomo, 1957.

Brande, Dorothea. Becoming a Writer. Los Angeles: Tarcher, 1981.

Bukowski, Charles. Hollywood. Santa Rosa: Ecco, 1989.

Caine, Michael. Acting in Film. New York: Applause, 2000.

Cayouette, Laura. Know Small Parts: An Actor's Guide to Turning Minutes into Moments and Moments into a Career. New Orleans: LA to NOLA P, 2012.

Coppola, Francis Ford. The Godfather Notebook. New York: Regan, 2016.

Corman, Roger. How I Made a Hundred Movies in Hollywood and Never Lost a Dime. New York: Delta, 1990.

Dunne, Will. The Dramatic Writer's Companion. Chicago: U of Chicago P, 2009.

Ebert, Roger. The Great Movies. New York: Broadway, 2002.

Egri, Lagos. The Art of Dramatic Writing. New York: Touchstone, 1972.

Elder, Robert K. The Film That Changed My Life. Chicago: Chicago Review, 2011.

Field, Syd. Screenplay: The Foundations of Screenwriting. New York: Dell, 1984.

Foster, Jack. How to Get Ideas. San Francisco: Berrett, 1996.

Gabler, Neal. An Empire of Their Own: How the Jews Invented Hollywood. New York: Anchor, 1989.

Goldman, William. Adventures in the Screen Trade. New York: Warner, 1984.

Grodin, Charles. It Would Be So Nice If You Weren't Here. New York: Vintage, 1989.

Kael, Pauline. 5001 Nights at the Movies. New York: Holt, 1991.

Keaton, Buster and Charles Samuels. My Wonderful World of Slapstick. New York: Da Capo, 1982.:

Krefft, Vanda. The Man Who Made the Movies: The Meteoric Rise and Tragic Fall of William Fox. New York: Harper, 2017.

Lumet, Sidney. Making Movies. New York: Vintage, 1996.

Mordden, Ethan. The Hollywood Studios. New York: Knopf, 1988.

Nowell-Smith, Geoffrey. The Oxford History of World Cinema. Oxford: Oxford UP, 1999.

Ovitz, Michael. Who is Michael Ovitz? New York: Portfolio, 2018.

Palestrant, Ellen. Conversations About Creativity. Scottsdale: Creative, 2018.

Schatz, Thomas. The Genius of the System: Hollywood Filmmaking in the Studio Era. New York: Holt, 1988.

Simens, Dov, S-S. From Reel to Deal: Everything You Need to Create a Successful Independent Film. New York: Warner, 2003.

Thomson, David. Warner Bros: The making of an America Movie Studio. New Haven: Yale UP, 2011.

Vance, Jeffrey. Chaplin: Genius of the Cinema. New York: Abrams, 2003.

Wellman, William. <u>A Short Time for Insanity</u>. New York: Hawthorn, 1974.

Wellman, William, Jr. <u>Wild Bill Wellman: Hollywood Rebel</u>. New York: Pantheon, 2015.

Wellman, William, Jr. <u>The Man and His Wings</u>. Westport: Praeger, 2006.

Wexman, Virginia Wright. <u>A History of Film</u>. White Plains: Pearson, 2009.

Must-See Movies

The African Queen

American Graffiti

Angels With Dirty Faces

Anna Christie

Apocalypse Now

Beat the Devil

The Big Lebowski

The Big Picture

Blonde Venus

Boyz N the Hood

Bram Stoker's Dracula

Bus Stop

The Caine Mutiny

Cape Fear

Carlito's Way

Casablanca

Chariots of Fire

Citizen Kane

Close Encounters of the Third Kind

College
The Color Purple
The Conversation
Cool Hand Luke
The Deer Hunter
The Defiant Ones
Deliverance
The Departed
The Devil Doll
Diner
Dracula
East of Eden
Frankenstein
Freaks
The Freshman
Gaslight
The General
Gentleman's Agreement
Ghost
Giant
The Goat
The Godfather

The Godfather Part II

The Godfather Part III

Gold Diggers of 1933

The Gold Rush

Gone With The Wind

Goodfellas

Guess Who's Coming to Dinner

The Grapes of Wrath

The Green Mile

The Heartbreak Kid

High Plains Drifter

Houdini

I Remember Mama

It Happened One Night

It's a Mad Mad Mad Mad World

It's a Wonderful Life

Judgment at Nuremberg

The Kid

King Kong

The King of Comedy

L.A. Confidential

La La Land

Léolo
Lifeboat
Like Water for Chocolate
Limelight
Little Caesar
The Long Kiss Goodnight
M
The Maltese Falcon
Man of a Thousand Faces
Man on the Flying Trapeze
The Man Who Knew Too Much
The Man Who Would Be King
Midnight Cowboy
Mighty Joe Young
The Miracle Worker
Modern Times
The Most Dangerous Game
My Dog Skip
My Little Chickadee
North By Northwest
Of Mice and Men
On the Waterfront

One, Two, Three

Only the Lonely

The Outlaw Josey Wales

The Outsiders

The Ox-Bow Incident

The Philadelphia Story

Play Misty For Me

The Player

The Pride of the Yankees

The Prince and the Showgirl

The Princess Bride

The Prizefighter and the Lady

The Public Enemy

The Purple Rose of Cairo

Queen Christina

Raging Bull

Raiders of the Lost Ark

Raising Arizona

Rear Window

Rebel Without a Cause

Requiem for a Heavyweight

The Roaring Twenties

Mike Kimmel

Rocky

Roman Holiday

Rope

Saving Private Ryan

Scarface

Scarlet Street

Schindler's List

Sea of Love

The Searchers

Sergeant York

Serpico

Se7en

The Shawshank Redemption

The Silence of the Lambs

Some Like it Hot

Speedy

A Star is Born

Story of G.I. Joe

Sullivan's Travels

Sunset Blvd.

Taxi Driver

Thelma & Louise

Trapeze

Unforgiven

The Unholy Three

The Unknown

The Untouchables

The Usual Suspects

U Turn

Valley of the Dolls

West Side Story

Westward the Women

Wild Bill: Hollywood Maverick

Wings

Yankee Doodle Dandy

Youth Without Youth

A Brief Glossary of Film Terms

Actor's Director. An actor's director devotes time to helping actors explore character analysis and motivations for each scene. They may rehearse extensively with their casts prior to filming, as well. They often come from a theater background, where lengthy rehearsals are the norm. Actors' directors may even schedule meetings between actors prior to casting them to evaluate their on-screen chemistry together.

In contrast, directors with a more technical orientation focus upon nuances of cinematography, including camera, lighting, sound design, and visual effects. These directors are often experienced camera operators who have been promoted to director. Not surprisingly, some actors express difficulty performing at their best when working with technically oriented directors. A common complaint is that these directors do not understand the actor's creative process in the same way that actors' directors do. Actors often say that technically oriented filmmakers are more comfortable directing equipment than people.

Backstory. This is the prior history of a character before we first meet that person on screen. This principle can also be applied to specific scenes or plot points in the script itself. Through the effective use of backstory, audiences may learn of prior, unseen events the filmmakers do not show us on screen. These prior events and motivations influence a character's subsequent actions as the storyline unfolds and gathers momentum.

Casting. The process of selecting and hiring actors for a motion picture, television show or other entertainment industry project.

Casting directors. These are the crew members tasked with seeking out talent and presenting the best available options (in their opinion) to directors and producers. Top casting directors have detailed knowledge of the actors in their geographic region and strong instincts for discovering new talent.

Close-up shot. The subject fills the screen and is framed very closely by the camera. This shot is intended to reveal a character's thought processes, subtle reactions, and moments of internal discovery. Close-up shots are also used on objects and parts of the body other than the face. Close-ups may thereby demonstrate danger or suspense (a hand reaching for a gun), or indicate important plot points non-verbally for the audience (a door being locked, a telephone line being cut).

Deus ex machina. This is a literary device developed in ancient Greece to deliver an unexpected resolution to a seemingly insurmountable problem or plot point. As used in the Greek theater, most notably by Euripides, Sophocles, and Aristophenes, one of the godlike characters from the Greek pantheon would arrive at the conclusion of the play to save the day. In the modern age, this technique is criticized for being overly simplistic and contrived. It is generally considered a sign of laziness and lack of creativity in writers.

Diegesis. This is Aristotle's description of a common writing technique to move stories forward. With this mechanism, authors reveal elements of their stories through verbal exposition, or *telling* the audience about specific prior events. Among the essays in this collection, Casablanca relies upon diegesis to advance the physical action of the story at a brisk pace. Critical plot points – such as the murder of Ugarte and the two German couriers – are delivered verbally, rather than visually.

Director. The crew member hired to oversee and coordinate every aspect of film production. The director supervises actor performance, cinematography, lighting, music, and also makes critical decisions about cutting or refining the screenplay while filming. Directors supervise editing after filming has been completed, as well. Film directors are hired for their artistic vision and commercial track record. Their job is considered the most prestigious and sought-after position in Hollywood. However, producers and studio executives may still fire them if production runs behind schedule, goes over-budget, or becomes otherwise problematic.

Interestingly, some directors have reputations as "actor's directors," while others are more comfortable with the technological side of filmmaking.

<u>Iris technique</u>. A highly visual means of opening and closing the camera lens with an expanding or contracting dark circle, thus mirroring the function of the iris inside the human eye. The technique was frequently used in the silent film era to begin or end a scene, but it was also sometimes used to highlight and direct the viewer's attention upon one specific detail or story element within the scene – like a spotlight.

<u>Jump cut</u>. Also called a <u>smash cut</u>, this technique is somewhat jarring to the audience, involving a rapid, unexpected camera movement from one character or scene to the next. It is used effectively in both comedy and drama, delivering highly visual sight gags, unforeseen storyline developments, and dramatic character reactions.

<u>Long shot</u>. Filming with the subject or characters placed at a far distance from the camera. This shot

is intended to reveal setting and locale, as well as the characters' relationship to their environment and one another.

Master shot. A film shot that includes every character in the scene. After editing, master shots are generally the first shots audiences see every time a new scene begins. This is important for clarity. Well-planned master shots help audiences understand the flow and direction of the storyline – and allow directors to advance the action seamlessly from one scene to the next.

Mimesis. This is another term derived from Aristotle and the ancient Greeks, and describes the techniques storytellers use to convey information visually, rather than verbally. It is the opposite process to diegesis. George Lucas leans heavily towards mimesis throughout Star Wars, clearly preferring to keep his characters' dialogue to a stark minimum. The Mos Eisley cantina scene, Luke's Jedi training aboard the Millennium Falcon, and the massive size of the Empire space vessel flying overhead in the film's opening sequence are all strong examples of mimesis.

Mise en scene. The manner in which a film director carefully frames all the visual elements and stages movement within the camera shot. Mise en scene is strategically used to set tone, establish environment, and create subtext in the film.

Producer. The crew member responsible for putting the entire film project together from concept to completion of photography. Producers raise money to finance films, and are ultimately responsible for hiring the entire cast and crew, including the director. In most cases, however, directors (particularly star-name directors) have near-total authority for decision-making on film sets.

There are several different types of producers, as well. An executive producer is the highest-ranking producer on a film. We sometimes see many different executive producers listed in film credits. This generally identifies producers with the resources and connections to fund feature films. In some cases, these are financiers or investors with little practical experience in filmmaking. Their experience in raising money, however, is invaluable to the project, and they are therefore rewarded with executive producer credits and compensation.

Screenplay. The written script for a motion picture. A well-formatted script should range from 90 to 120 pages in length. One written page of a screenplay generally translates to one minute of performance time on screen.

Tracking shot. A technique in which directors move their cameras to follow actors or objects that are also moving. The film camera is securely attached to a wheeled dolly for stability and fluidity of movement. A camera operator is seated at the dolly, as well. The name of this shot is derived from the actual lengths of track (similar to railroad tracks) cameras glide along to follow and capture the physical action. Tracking shots are generally used to heighten dramatic tension and convey a more active sense of movement and suspense.

About Henry Hoffman

Dr. Henry Hoffman holds a B.A. from California State University at Fullerton, and an M.A. from Illinois State University at Normal. He also holds two advanced doctoral degrees. Dr. Hoffman earned his first Ph.D. in Philosophy from the University of New Mexico at Albuquerque. He earned a second Ph.D. in Film Studies from Wayne State University in Detroit, Michigan.

Henry studied acting with Harold Clurman at The Actors Studio. He also studied directing with both Peter Brook and Edward Duerr. He completed advanced studies in textual analysis of William Shakespeare's work with Joseph Chaiken. Henry studied Critical Theory with Dr. John Kirk and trained personally under Werner Erhard, as well.

He was a leading actor with many premiere regional stages, including the Mark Taper Forum, Colorado Shakespeare Festival (Boulder), A Contemporary Theatre (Seattle), PlayMakers Repertory Company (North Carolina), Berkeley Repertory Theatre, and the American Conservatory Theatre (A.C.T.). As a performer, he has worked with some of the aristocrats of the profession, including

Dame Eileen Atkins, Jose Ferrer, Jack O'Brien, William Ball, Ellis Rabb, and Salome Jens.

As an educator, Dr. Hoffman has taught at the American Conservatory Theatre, American Academy of Dramatic Arts, Shakespeare Theatre of New Jersey, University of North Carolina at Chapel Hill, New Orleans Center for Creative Arts, and the California State Universities at San Jose and Chico. He has directed Equity stage productions in both New York and Los Angeles. Dr. Hoffman currently directs teenage actors in the Young Shakespeare Company. In 2002, he was named one of the twenty leading educators in the United States by <u>USA Today</u>, earning him a position on the newspaper's All USA Teacher Team.

Excerpts from Dr. Hoffman's forthcoming book <u>Tyrone Power: A Luminous Pause</u> have been published in <u>Xavier Review</u> of New Orleans.

About Mike Kimmel

Mike Kimmel is a film, television, stage and commercial actor, acting coach, and college instructor. He is a twenty-plus year member of SAG-AFTRA with extensive experience in both the New York and Los Angeles markets. He has worked with directors Francis Ford Coppola, Robert Townsend, Craig Shapiro, and Christopher Cain among many others. TV credits include Game of Silence, Zoo, Treme, In Plain Sight, Cold Case, Breakout Kings, Memphis Beat, and Buffy The Vampire Slayer. He was a regular sketch comedy player on The Tonight Show, performing live on stage and in pre-taped segments with Jay Leno for eleven years.

Mike has appeared in dozens of theatrical plays on both coasts, including Radio City Music Hall, Equity Library Theater, Stella Adler Theater, Double Image Theater, The Village Gate, and Theater at the Improv. He trained with Michael Shurtleff, William Hickey, Ralph Marrero, Gloria Maddox, Harold Sylvester, Wendy Davis, Amy Hunter, Bob Collier, and Stuart Robinson. He holds a B.A. from Brandeis University and an M.A. from California State University at Dominguez Hills.

As an educator, he has taught at Upper Iowa University, University of New Orleans, University of Phoenix, Glendale Community College, Nunez Community College, Delgado Community College, and in the Los Angeles, Beverly Hills, and Burbank, California public school districts. He is a two-time past president of New Orleans Toastmasters, the public speaking organization, and often serves as an international speech contest judge. Mike has written and collaborated on numerous scripts for stage and screen. <u>In Lincoln's Footsteps</u>, his full-length historical drama on Presidents Lincoln and Garfield, was a 2013 semi-finalist in the National Playwrights Conference at the Eugene O'Neill Theater Center. He is the 2014 recipient of the Excellence in Teaching Award from Upper Iowa University.

Mike is a full voting member of the National Academy of Television Arts and Sciences, the organization that produces the Emmy Awards. He is the author of <u>Scenes for Teens</u>, <u>Acting Scenes for Kids and Tweens</u>, <u>Monologues for Teens</u>, and <u>Monologues for Kids and Tweens</u>. He is also featured in Francis Ford Coppola's 2017 book, <u>Live Cinema</u>.

"You know what your problem is, it's that you haven't seen enough movies – all of life's riddles are answered in the movies."

– Steve Martin

www.ingramcontent.com/pod-product-compliance
Lightning Source LLC
Chambersburg PA
CBHW070613010526
44118CB00012B/1504